P9-DGB-273

FINDING GOD

FINDING GOD

DR. LARRY CRABB, JR.

ZondervanPublishingHouse
Grand Rapids, Michigan
A Division of HarperCollins*Publishers*

Finding God
Copyright © 1993 by Lawrence J. Crabb, Jr., Ph.D., P.A., dba, Institute of Biblical Counseling

Requests for information should be addressed to:
Zondervan Publishing House
Grand Rapids, Michigan 49530

ISBN 0-310-59430-8

All Scripture quotations, unless otherwise noted, are taken from the *Holy Bible, New International Version®. NIV®.* Copyright © 1973, 1978, 1984, by International Bible Society. Used by permission of Zondervan Publishing House. All rights reserved.

All rights reserved. No part of this publication may be reproduced, stored in a retrieval system, or transmitted in any form or by any means—electronic, mechanical, photocopy, recording, or any other—except for brief quotations in printed reviews, without the prior permission of the publisher.

Published in association with Sealy M. Yates, Literary Agent, Orange, CA.

Edited by Sandra L. Vander Zicht
Interior design by Bob Hudson
Cover design by John M. Lucas

Printed in the United States of America

To the memory of Dr. Charles Smith, a mentor who prayed for his cancer to return if it would bring him closer to God. In his last year, he found God in a measure he had never known before. And then he died—of cancer.

To my students who have studied with me in the master's program in biblical counseling. You have taught me more than any other group about walking the painful path toward finding God.

Contents

III. THE PATHWAY TO FINDING GOD

Acknowledgments

Thanks to an office staff (Susan Rike, Sandy Pierce, Shirley Bowling, Natalie Merilatt, Cheryl Jones) who graciously endure my shifting moods and still believe in me.

Thanks to Cheryl Jones and Sandy Pierce for typing, retyping, and retyping again—and for the support I felt through it all.

Thanks to my colleagues—Dan Allender, Tom Varney, Al Andrews, Liam Atchison, Don Hudson, Kim Hutchins—for providing a community that thinks without too quickly evaluating and that respects the directions my mind takes me.

Thanks to Sandy Vander Zicht for her editorial work. I've felt buoyed by her belief in this project and by the hard work she has done to make this book as good as it can be. Thanks too to Scott Bolinder and the Zondervan team for their encouragement in so many areas of my ministry.

Thanks to Sealy Yates, my friend and agent who I know is for me—that means a lot.

Thanks to my parents—Larry and Isabel Crabb—for realistically displaying a life of pursuing God that has impacted me in more ways and with more depth than a thousand books could describe.

Thanks to the many older saints whose lives reflect the truths about finding God that I barely grasp; among them James Hatch, Hunter Norwood, Pamela Reeve, Broughton Knox, John Bramhall, and my parents-in-law Howard and Helen Lankford.

And more thanks than could ever be expressed to my wife, Rachael. My pursuit of God is not a smooth one. She feels all the bumps with me—and still wants to walk with me on the path. I have no clearer illustration of grace.

A Personal Note

L et me tell you why I wrote this book.
I have come to a place in my life where I need to know God
better or I won't make it. Life at times has a way of throwing me
into such blinding confusion and severe pain that I lose all
hope. Joy is gone. Nothing encourages me.

Perhaps the most important lesson I learn as I go through
dark seasons is this: *there is no escape in this life from pain and
problems.* I can live obediently, practice spiritual disciplines,
and claim my identity in Christ, but problems still continue.

More than anything else, I need a *person to trust,* someone
who can give me hope, joy, and peace in the midst of life's
unpredictable struggles. A *plan to follow* is not enough.
Applying biblical principles does not always make things
happen as I want. Without someone to trust, I must either
pretend things are better than they are or live to relieve pain.
And if neither denial nor efforts to relieve pain do the job, I
will end my life through immorality or craziness or suicide.

The rhetoric we're all used to—"just trust the Lord, pray
more, get counseling, follow God's plan more carefully"—must
give way to the reality of finding God.

I wrote this book in response to the desperate cry of my
heart to know God better. More than ever before, I am
convinced that God yearns to be known by us far more than we
want to know him, and his great work in us is to increase our
passion for knowing him until it is stronger than all other
passions. Developing that passion in our hearts is a long,
difficult process to which God is relentlessly committed. The
way is hard, the road less traveled than others, but the journey
is worth it. God is immeasurably good, and he can be trusted!

As I share my journey through my problems toward finding God, I fervently hope that a passion to know God will be stirred within you, perhaps a deeper passion than you've ever known before.

With joyful hope,

Larry Crabb

FINDING GOD

Introduction:
Solving Problems Isn't the Point

George MacDonald once began a sermon by saying, "If I cannot persuade you to understand a little more of Jesus Christ, my labor is lost in coming to you. If I cannot help any human heart to draw closer to the living one, my labor is lost."

He went on to ask, "Did the fact ever cross your mind that you are here in this world just to understand the Lord Jesus Christ, and for no other reason?"

In this book, I want to look for the path that will bring us closer to God. If I were to write this twenty years from now, it would be a far better book. But reporting stages along the journey toward finding God has value. Graduate physicists may never think about what they learned in seventh-grade math, not because basic math has become irrelevant to them, but because they have learned it well enough to assume it rather than to study it.

If you are chewing on spiritual meat that would break my undeveloped teeth but provides you with nourishment I have not yet known, then perhaps this book will bring back memories from days gone by and will warm your heart with appreciation for how far God has brought you.

If you are still struggling to memorize the alphabet of basic Christian truths, I invite you to look ahead. Don't be ashamed of where you are. Dream a bit. Imagine where God's Spirit wants to take you. You may skip a grade, but don't plan on it. Learn whatever the Master Teacher puts before you. Trust him to guide you unerringly through a curriculum specially designed for you that, after much discouragement and failure, will qualify you to one day receive your diploma from the hand of Christ. We are here to know the Lord Jesus Christ—there is no other reason for living.

FINDING GOD OR FINDING OURSELVES

In today's world we have shifted away from finding God toward finding ourselves. Fondness for ourselves has become the highest virtue, and self-hatred the greatest sin.

It all began innocently enough. The church became aware of the terrible pain of its people, a pain that darkened their souls like a thick fog, keeping out the bright and joyful warmth of knowing Christ. The church had to face the uncomfortable fact that the followers of Christ, who of all people on earth should be happy, were often miserable—pressured and discontent, not liking God, themselves, or anyone else.

In our search for explanations, we discovered that wounds from childhood are deep, and that time does not always heal. The normal activities of Christian community—going to church, studying the Bible, praying, and working in the food pantry—don't provide a sufficient remedy. Beneath cheerful fellowship, many people suffer desperate loneliness, bitter self-hatred, and a chronic awareness of not measuring up that only gets worse with increased efforts to do right.

One school of thought tells us that feeling hurt and longing to feel better is selfish. Students in this school warn against preoccupation with self and the corrupting influence of psychology. They insist that trying to understand our thirst-driven passions and desires is an ungodly concession to "pagan" psychology. They further declare that healing personal wounds and restoring a sense of enjoyable identity is rubbish—dangerous, humanistic rubbish.

These people are wrong! Powerful, painful, deceiving forces within us are crying out to be understood, sorted through, and handled. When we obey God out of duty, stifling our feelings of pain and confusion, we miss something vital about what it means to relate to Christ. A firm belief in the sufficiency of Christ and his Word does not mean we have to look away from our ugly memories or deep wounds. Our Lord invites us to come to him as we are, pretending about nothing, feeling our pain, admitting our rage, and longing to satisfy our souls with rich food.

Thankfully, many have heard our Lord's invitation to come as we are, with an ache in our souls that won't go away. As never before, the church is aware that its people are in pain. But this welcome sensitivity has backfired. Rather than drawing us closer to God and freeing us to care more deeply about others, this sensitivity has made us more aware of how intensely we long to feel better about *ourselves* and more determined to find ways to do so! The spotlight has fallen on us as abused, wounded, needy people, and God has been cast as the great Higher Power, waiting in the wings for his cue to come heal our hurts and restore us to responsible living.

---

*Feeling better has become more important
to us than finding God.*

Helping people to feel loved and worthwhile has become the central mission of the church. We are learning not to worship God in self-denial and costly service, but to embrace our inner child, heal our memories, overcome addictions, lift our depressions, improve our self-images, establish self-preserving boundaries, substitute self-love for self-hatred, and replace shame with an affirming acceptance of who we are.

Recovery from pain is absorbing an increasing share of the church's energy. And that is alarming. Although the gospel does bless us with a new identity that was meant to be enjoyed, it calls us to higher values than self-acceptance, values like turning the other cheek, esteeming others as greater than ourselves, going the second mile, enduring rejection and persecution, living not for the pleasures of this life but for those of the next one, and clinging to the promises of God when we don't feel his goodness. But these higher values, the kind that make people of whom the world is not worthy (Heb. 11:38), have fallen on hard times.

We have become committed to relieving the pain behind our problems rather than using our pain to wrestle more passionately with the character and purposes of God. *Feeling better has become more important than finding God.* And worse, we assume that people who find God always feel better.

As a result, we happily camp on biblical ideas that help us to feel loved and accepted, and we pass over Scripture that calls us to higher ground. We twist wonderful truths about God's acceptance, his redeeming love, and our new identity in Christ into a basis for honoring ourselves rather than seeing those truths for what they are: the stunning revelation of a God gracious enough to love people who hated him, a God worthy to be honored above everyone and everything else.

We have learned to praise God the way we tip a specially attentive waiter. Good treatment we expect, but exceptional treatment deserves special recognition. And certainly God qualifies for extra notice: he has gone to great trouble to feed our souls and bolster our self-esteem. We therefore leave him a big tip, feeling benevolent and noble, and he, in turn, beams with humble appreciation as he hears us say, "Well done! You have served us well."

But this is backwards! We have rearranged things so that God is now worthy of honor *because* he has honored us. "Worthy is the Lamb," we cry, not in response to his amazing grace, but because he has recovered what we value most: the ability to like ourselves. *We now matter more than God.*

A THIRD WAY

Modern Christians are presented with two options for dealing with our lives: Either we can understand how our souls have been wounded and how to receive God's healing nourishment, or we can obey God as we would a stern, uninvolved father, and never tell him how bad we hurt. Either our hurt is the point, or it is no point at all. Either our needs matter more than anything else, or it is wrong even to mention them.

We need a third way of handling our lives—a way that combines a passionate sensitivity to our deepest struggles with a tender insistence that something matters more than how we feel. It is healthy to face the pain in our souls, to feel bad when others violate our dignity, to admit to ourselves how desperately we long to feel loved and valued and accepted as we are. But, in the middle of all this, we need to remember that the point of Christianity is not us, but the God who cares for us.

Our hunger does not obligate God. He is not a waiter who, at the snap of our fingers, runs out of heaven's kitchen loaded down with trays of food to fill our empty stomachs. With his blood Christ purchased a people for God and made us priests to serve him (Rev. 5:9–10). We exist for *him*, not the other way around.

But bowing before God, living for his pleasure rather than for ours, does not reduce us to slaves whose personal feelings do not matter. God cares about our hurts. He wants us to enjoy our new identity as unique, forgiven, valuable men and women with something important to contribute. How we feel, how we've been treated, what we do, why we do it—everything about our lives is important. We are valuable players in the cosmic drama he directs, and we are not wrong to be concerned with how we're getting on.

But God matters more. He invites us to enter into relationship with him on his terms. He invites us to join him in achieving his great purpose: the overthrowing of evil and the bringing together of all things in Christ. He invites us, in short, to find *him*. And he lets us know that in the process of finding him, we'll find ourselves.

We must, however, do more than superficially agree that finding God is a higher priority than solving our problems. Somehow that purpose must reach into our hearts in the same way that cancer spreads through the body, destroying everything in its way. Until the reality of God crowds out every other reality, until we are moved to know him with a passion that we feel nowhere else, we will not use the struggles of life as an impetus to find God. Until our passion for finding God is deeper than any other passion, we will arrange life according to *our* taste, not God's.

These truths are not academic for me. God has brought a severe mercy into my life to deepen my awareness of the need to seek him. Let me tell my story.

I
THE IMPORTANCE OF
FINDING GOD

1
A Personal Journey

On Sunday, March 3, 1991, at 9:55 A.M., a United Airlines 737 bound for the airport in Colorado Springs crashed nose first into a neighborhood park, killing all twenty-five people on board.

My older brother, Bill, was on that plane.

My wife, Rachael, and I were sitting in church when an elder tapped me on the shoulder. "You have an emergency phone call," he whispered. I followed him to the church office and pressed the blinking button on the telephone.

"Hello?" I said.

"Larry? This is Dad. Bill's been in an accident. Phoebe just called from the airport. We don't know how bad it is, but she's really shaken up. Could you get down there?"

I returned to the sanctuary and whispered to Rachael that we had to leave. The elder who had summoned me met us at the door. I told him what had happened, and he looked at me with deep compassion. That was the first time I broke down.

When we arrived at the Colorado Springs airport, an hour's drive from our church in Denver, people were everywhere. The usual airport bustle seemed more frantic. I stopped a uniformed airport official and asked what had happened.

"Flight 585 has crashed just north of the airport. There are no survivors."

I walked outside the terminal, stood by the curb, and simply said to my wife, "Bill is dead." An emptiness I had never known before descended like a heavy weight on my heart.

A FRIGHTENING PASSION

I cried many times during those first two weeks after the plane crash, and I still break down occasionally when something reminds me of the terrible loss our family has suffered.

But two weeks after the accident, I sensed tears that had not yet been shed, tears pressing for release from an even deeper source than the profound loss I felt over Bill's death. I told my wife something strange was going on inside me. A frightening passion was being stirred. Quiet tremors—the early signs of an impending earthquake—shook my soul.

During the day on Sunday, March 17, I felt restless, uneasy. That night, I couldn't sleep. At midnight, I slipped out of bed, reached for my Bible, and headed for the privacy of my study.

For reasons still unclear, within seconds of my sitting down the dam burst. Tears gushed from my eyes and poured down my face. I sobbed, I wailed, I heaved for perhaps twenty minutes, without one recognizable word coming from my mouth, just the groaning of a soul in wrenching pain. I felt an unspeakable sorrow beyond any I had ever known. With terrible clarity, I realized that I, along with everyone else, was out of the Garden of Eden and had no way back in.

And then words began to come, out loud, subdued at first, then with the intensity of a scream. I cried to the Lord, "I cannot endure what I know to be true. Life is painful. I am selfish. Everything is intolerable. Nothing satisfies. Nothing brings relief. Nothing good is certain. There is no rest. Sorrow outweighs joy. I cannot go on without knowing you better."

Then, as suddenly as they had begun, the tears stopped. I sat quietly, aware that I was doing business with God, that my deepest being was engaged with him. He must be pleased, I thought, with my zealous longing for communion with him.

I felt good for perhaps a minute. And then, with the impact of a battering ram, the realization hit me: "I am preoccupied with *me!* I'm not even close to touching God. He's not on my mind. *I* am!" The tears flowed again, this time with even greater violence.

My body writhed in pain as I cried out: "God, I don't know how to come to you. I need to know you, to sense your presence, to feel your love, more than anything else. But I don't know what to do. Every path I follow leads back to me. I must find the way to you! I know you're all I have. *But I don't know you well enough for you to be all I need.* Please let me find you."

If ever I hoped for a vision or an audible voice speaking from the silence of heaven, it was then. But nothing came. No soft glow filled the room. No voice disrupted my solitude. I sat alone. And, involuntarily, I again became quiet.

The tears were gone, the spring from which they came utterly dried up. I felt limp, still desperate but not frantic, beyond the reach of anyone but God.

After sitting for another few minutes in exhaustion, I numbly reached for my Bible. I laid it on my lap, staring at it, wondering where to turn.

I recalled my words less than ten minutes earlier, "I need to know you, but I don't know what to do," and my mind drifted, at first casually, then compellingly, to the words of Hebrews 11:6: "And without faith it is impossible to please God, because anyone who comes to him must believe that he exists and that he rewards those who earnestly seek him."

I turned to those words in my Bible and read them four or five times. They fascinated me, partly because I knew that they had power, a power I was certain I would eventually know.

Long ago I gave up hope of ever finding a single key to the Christian life that, once found, would forever remain in my hands and would, on demand, open the doors to the mysteries of heaven. But that night I knew that Jesus Christ was a real person, that heaven was a real place, and that the Christian life was supernatural. I sensed that, although I was not about to stumble on final and ultimate truth, there was something important for me to consider in that passage, something that God intended to show me to guide me toward knowing him.

I went back to bed with no fresh insights into that verse in Hebrews, but with a strange, almost exhilarating confidence that treasures were waiting to be mined, that I would uncover liberating truths perfectly suited to my need to know God.

FINDING GOD

For the next several weeks, that verse haunted me. I couldn't get it out of my head. I read the words again, pondered them, studied their context, reflected on all that I knew from Scripture about how an already forgiven soul comes to God, and I prayed for wisdom.

The ideas that formed in my mind during that time of reflection are the foundation for this book. They aren't terribly new—they're as old as the text—but they seem fresh to me. Certain things seem clearer to me now, important things that need to control our understanding of life.

I invite you to walk with me along the path I followed in trying to understand what God is saying in that text and throughout the whole Bible. Only Christians can walk this path, only people who rest in the undeserved and surprising forgiveness of God, only people who have learned to recognize and despise their hatred of God as the ugliest, most troublesome reality in their souls.

How can an unmarried man or woman struggling with loneliness find God? How can a bereaved parent enjoy God's goodness? How can a bankrupt businessman with a large family rest in what he knows about God? How can a discouraged, confused, and unmotivated teenager find enough confidence in God to continue living? Think with me about what the writer to the Hebrews is saying to people who want to find God.

2
There's More to Life Than Merely Living

T heology becomes rich only when it survives the onslaught of pain. And sound theology leads us through our pain to a fuller experience of Christ, and therefore of hope and love and joy.*

The pain that opens our hearts to search for God is deep. It is not the peevish pain of a grumbler who mutters or mumbles in discontent. It is not the angry pain of a narcissist who finds out that self-centeredness has consequences. It is not the usual psychological hurt we hear so much about today that creates a

---

*The gripping message of the Bible will never be fully heard in the library. When we value scholarly precision and doctrinal purity above a personally transforming encounter with the God who reveals himself in his Word, when we fail to see that an academic grasp of Scripture often leads to a proud appreciation of knowledge more than a humble and passionate appreciation of Christ, we develop an orthodoxy that crushes life. And we miss the gospel that frees us to live.

In order to catch the pulse of Scripture and hear the heartbeat of God, we must be actively grappling with the overwhelming reality of what life is like outside the Garden of Eden. If we numb our souls to the ongoing struggles with sin and disappointment that fallen people living in a fallen world experience, then our time in the Bible will yield puffy knowledge rather than liberating truth.

thirst for nothing more than liking ourselves better and enjoying life more.

Rather, it is the pain of someone who wants to enjoy pleasures he cannot find and who fears that misery seems inevitable and perhaps deserved. It is pain that makes us stand still and think about something outside of ourselves, something more important and more interesting than our concerns about who we are and how we're getting on. It is pain that compels us to ask terrifying questions about life and God.

The pain that leads to sound theology is something like the experience of a man walking through an old house at midnight. Hearing a noise, he stops short. He stands motionless, every nerve alert to the presence of an unseen host.

Only the frightening, immobilizing, and awe-inspiring realization that we are out of the Garden with no way back in and that supernatural powers hover about us will stop us long enough to hear what is beyond our immediate experience. Only that dreadful awareness will create an alertness that enables us to hear God speak through his Word to introduce us to an unmistakably new dimension of life.

This kind of pain filled me the night I read Hebrews 11:6. I *wanted* to hear God. I *needed* to hear God. Nothing mattered more to me than finding him. I was engaged in a far more important mission than preparing a sermon or getting together some thoughts for a book. I was struggling to find a way to live.

With the passion of a deer panting for streams of water, I plunged into Hebrews 11:6, looking for God: "And without faith it is impossible to please him, because anyone who comes to him must believe that he exists and that he rewards those who earnestly seek him."

THREE INTERRUPTIONS

Eager to understand the context of this text, I read the entire chapter, a narrative of the lives of many Old Testament heroes of the faith. The first thing that struck me was that

Hebrews 11 is interrupted three times by a briefly stated principle or observation. The first interruption (v. 6) details what it means to come to God. The second (vv. 13–16) announces that these Old Testament heroes of the faith were longing for a better country—a heavenly one. The third, at the end of the chapter (vv. 38–40), affirms that "God had planned something better."

As I pondered the author's inspired decision to insert each principle in its place, I wondered if the people mentioned just before the principle illustrated its point. If so, the writer to the Hebrews was saying something like this: "If you want to understand what I said in verse six, you should look back to the person whose life made me think of the principle I stated in that verse. When I spoke of coming to God, pleasing him by faith, believing that he is who he says he is, and trusting him to reward you in due time, I was thinking of Enoch. Study Enoch's life to understand what it takes to come to God—and to find him!"

I knew that I could not survive life outside the Garden unless I knew God better. The battle raging in my soul was one I knew I could not win. Either I had to deny how painful things were (but a God whom we can find only by denying realities that undermine our confidence in him is not worth knowing); or I could numb my pain with the temporary thrills of sin (but short-term pleasure brings long-term misery); or I could hope that my obedience might persuade God to bless me with good health, plenty of money, successful relationships, and few hassles (but God does not function like a vending machine that delivers the candy I select when I deposit the right coins).

I needed to come to God on *his* terms. I took hope from God's words to his suffering people during Jeremiah's day: "You will seek me and find me when you seek me with all your heart. I will be found by you, declares the LORD" (Jer. 29:13–14).

But what does it mean to seek God with all my heart? Greater efforts to obey? Less television? Increased giving? Leading another Bible study? More regular devotional times? A lengthier prayer list? Listening only to Christian radio? More witnessing? Fewer purchases? Improved cooperation with demanding employees? An all-night prayer vigil?

How could I come to God confident that I would find him in the manner he is willing and eager to be found? I decided to look at Enoch's life for help.

ENOCH WALKED WITH GOD

I turned to the first mention of Enoch in the Bible, Genesis 5:18–24. Genesis 5 records one of those genealogies that are so tempting to skip or to read through quickly. But read the entire chapter carefully and see if anything stands out.

Notice that ten men are listed in that chapter, starting with Adam, continuing through Seth, and ending with Noah. In each case, with the regularity of a formula, the Bible states that after the man became a father, he lived a certain number of years. Underscore that word *lived* in verses 4, 7, 10, 13, 16, 19, 26, and 30. Every man is said to have "lived" from the time he became a father to the day he was buried, except Noah (whose death comes later in the story) and Enoch.

Notice verse 22. "And after he became the father of Methuselah, Enoch walked with God 300 years." The other men merely lived. Enoch *walked with God.* The contrast is worth noting.

How is "walking with God" distinct from "living out" your allotted years? Perhaps if I am to come to God and actually find him, I must first ask the question: Am I merely living, or am I walking with God? (The prospect of walking with God continues to stagger me. Sometimes the possibility seems remote: Enoch was a biblical character; I'm only a twentieth-century American. At other times, it dawns on me with a force that takes my breath away—I, too, could really walk with God!)

The prophet Amos asked the question, "Do two walk together unless they have agreed to do so?" (Amos 3:3). If I am to walk with God, one thing is immediately clear: we must go in the same direction. And God doesn't negotiate. He invites me to join him. He will not go with me on my side trips.

God's course is clear. He has committed himself to bringing "all things in heaven and on earth together under one head, even Christ" (Eph. 1:10). If I want to walk with him, I have no option but to join him on that path. Agreeing to join him requires that every other ambition in my heart become secondary to promoting Christ. Anything that contradicts this purpose must be abandoned.

Those terms are demanding. Following Christ requires something of us—more than rejoicing in our new identity. Sometimes it feels like we have to give up our only hope for life.

I once spoke with a woman whose husband regularly struck their teenage son. The boy was terrified of his father and had given up his faith because God was doing nothing to protect him from his father's wrath. The mother was heartbroken, confused, and angry. She asked me for help.

She told me that her mother had died when she was ten years old, and four years later her father had taken his own life. The care of her three younger siblings fell entirely on her fourteen-year-old shoulders. Over the years, she had become an intensely responsible woman, determined to solve everyone's problems, including her own.

As we chatted, I sensed she was listening with an attitude of resigned condescension: "Thanks for your willingness to help. I will consider what you say, but I'm fully aware that no one can really help. No one is strong or caring enough, and the responsibility to figure out what I must do is mine and mine alone." She did not say this aloud, but her attitude clearly conveyed this meaning.

At one point, I suggested that she had cast herself in the role of survivor. She saw herself as the leader of a camping expedition lost in the wilderness with a blizzard raging. Everything depended on her. Her one goal was to gather together her considerable resources—she was an extremely capable woman—and see to it that everybody got out safely.

With that resolution locked deeply in her soul, her questions, "How can I help my son?" and "What can I do with my husband?" reflected a clenched-fist determination to make life work better. Beneath that passion-filled agenda was a lonely cry for someone to be there for her, to love her in a way that would free her to go off duty as the leader of the endangered expedition. But when anyone did come through for her, as I wanted to, she immediately saw the weaknesses in that person's approach and went back to work.

Her agenda was to fix her world until it could properly take care of her. *God's* agenda is to bring all things together in Christ until every knee bows before him. These two persons— my counselee and God—were not walking together. They were moving in different directions. She came to God not to walk with him, but to persuade him to supply the energy and power she needed to fulfill her purposes. Until she changed direction, she would know neither peace in the situation nor wisdom for dealing with it.

Enoch walked with God. It became clear that if I wanted to come to God as Enoch did, I needed more than a simple prayer of commitment and a few extra efforts to discipline myself into spiritual shape. Surgery without anesthesia was called for, radical surgery that would cut out every demand that things go my way. And, incredibly, I *wanted* to submit to that operation. It seemed wise to permit an experienced Surgeon— one whose patients always recovered—to go to work on my fatal disease.

But the surgical process, I realized, was not easy. Not only must I consciously commit myself to purity of purpose, I must renew that commitment regularly, especially when the pain in my heart screams for relief. And I must become familiar with the firmly entrenched and loathsome energy within me that easily justifies stepping over moral lines to bring some comfort to my aching soul. When I realize that my commitment to self is fueled by angry doubts that God cannot be trusted to do for me what needs doing, then a spirit of repentance develops, a willingness to turn away from self-centered purposes in order to seek God.

Our agenda is to fix the world until it can properly take care of us. God's agenda is to bring all things together in Christ until every knee bows before him.

The surgery, however, is not over in a day. Rather, the Surgeon follows me around with knife in hand, gently pointing out further evidence of my disease of self-ism and waiting for me to lie still enough for another incision. The surprising effect of this surgery is that I now give more energy to pursuing God's purposes and to watching out for contrary agendas within me. I still grieve when others mistreat me, but as I submit to the Surgeon, I grieve more over my weak commitment to Christ than over whatever harsh treatment I may endure, and I rejoice more over the Lord's kindness than I do over my bolstered self-esteem.

Anyone who comes to God must come as Enoch came, consciously surrendering his life to eternal purposes, fully aware that God does not always guarantee the immediate comfort of his children.

MORE APPALLED BY UNHOLINESS THAN BY DISCOMFORT

A second observation about Enoch is that, unlike the vast majority of people in his day and ours, he was bothered more when he saw folks acting selfishly than when he saw them hurting. Jude records the only sermon preached by Enoch in Scripture. In this sermon, Enoch railed against people who valued immediate comfort and pleasure over personal holiness:

"See, the Lord is coming with thousands upon thousands of his holy ones to judge everyone, and to convict all the ungodly of all the ungodly acts they have done in the ungodly way, and of all the harsh words ungodly sinners have spoken against him" (Jude 14, 15).

The problem in Enoch's day, in Jude's, and in our own is the same. We treat personal discomfort (self-hatred, low self-esteem, insomnia, money pressures, loneliness) as the central evil from which we need to be saved. When we blend the pursuit of comfort with Christianity, Jesus becomes a divine masseur whose demands we heed only after we are properly relaxed.

But that is not the Christianity of the Bible. Christ offers hope, not relief, in the middle of suffering, and he commands us to pursue him hotly even when we'd rather stop and look after our own well-being.

Enoch warned us about speaking harsh words against God. Perhaps nothing makes us grumble quite like personal suffering which seems clearly unjust and to which God seems indifferent.

A friend of mine met his wife in Bible college. He decided to marry her only if it were clearly God's will. He prayed fervently, counseled with godly people, sought his parents' advice, and maintained the highest moral standards during their courtship. With the warm approval of everyone involved, he asked her to marry him, and the two of them agreed to give their lives to Christian service.

After seven years of marriage and the birth of two children, his wife told him that she was a lesbian and wanted to live with the lover she had been seeing secretly for several years. She left her family, divorced her husband, moved in with her female companion—and six years later took her own life. Since then the man's two children, now teenagers, have developed serious problems. His daughter is both bulimic and promiscuous; his son recently admitted to a drug habit that started when he was ten.

Suppose this man asks you for help. After he recounts the

tragic details of his life and weeps openly for his children and dead wife, he cries out, "Why didn't God do anything? Why did he let me marry her when all it caused was heartbreak and suffering? I earnestly sought his will and look what happened. How can I trust him with the rest of my life? Everything is ruined. I have no guarantee that my children will ever straighten out, and I have no reason to believe that my wife is anywhere but in hell!"

If you subscribe to the theology of Job's comforters, you'll help this man no more than they helped Job. To get God to give you what you want, Job's friends said, present your case before God, live as you should, repent of all evil, and God "will rouse himself on your behalf and restore you to your rightful place" (Job 8:6).

When I am not convinced that God is good, I will quietly—but with tight-lipped resolve—take over responsibility for my own well-being.

In our day, the message sounds like this: you can maneuver God to get what you want. God will not resurrect your wife, and he may not straighten out your kids, but he will help you feel good about who you are. Even if your hard circumstances do not change, you can accept yourself and enjoy who you are.

We moderns no longer err by defining the peace of God that passes all understanding as pleasant circumstances. Our mistake is to think that peace means having a satisfying sense of our own value and worth. *Neither* definition gets to the heart of the matter. God's peace belongs to those who have confidence in his goodness even when life is tough and their self-esteem is low. It should be noted that we can experience God's peace *and* a poor self-image at the same time.

When I am not convinced that God is good, and when I underestimate the seriousness of my struggle to believe in his goodness, I will quietly—but with tight-lipped resolve—take over responsibility for my own well-being. And I will regard God's love for me as reason to work hard at loving myself. I think, "God loves me. He fully accepts me. He wants me to enjoy who I am as his child. Therefore, increasing my enjoyment of my own identity is central to his plan."

Jude called people who "change the grace of our God into a license for immorality" (Jude 4) "godless men." Do not think of godlessness and immorality as only the obvious sins like adultery, cheating, or drunkenness. *Whenever we place a higher priority on solving our problems than on pursuing God, we are immoral.*

The battle my friend faces is to believe that God is worthy to be trusted even though he did not prevent his wife from committing suicide, his daughter from becoming bulimic and promiscuous, and his son from taking drugs. If he loses this battle, my friend will be far more offended by how bad things have turned out in his life than by his unholy demand for happiness. If he wins this battle, he will be freed *from* trying to salvage some happiness from the rubble of his life and freed *to* devote himself to God's purposes and to discover—if only in glimpses—the meaning of real joy.

Whenever we place a higher priority on solving our problems than on pursuing God, we are immoral.

We must call God good even when we suffer—because he is! And, when things are going well, we must call him good for reasons that go beyond our immediate blessings. Otherwise, when we hurt, we will speak harshly against God, and we will continue to do whatever it takes to satisfy our souls. *We will be more troubled by our discomfort than by our unholiness.*

If I am to come to God and find him, then I must come as Enoch came, believing that he is good no matter what life brings and refusing to pursue comfort at the expense of my commitment to honor him.

ENOCH VERSUS LAMECH

Look again at Jude 14. Jude introduces Enoch as the "seventh from Adam." No doubt his primary reason for doing so was to distinguish this Enoch from the other Enochs mentioned in the Bible.

But, in my desire to understand all I could about coming to God from the example of Enoch, I wondered if further lessons might be learned from this phrase. I therefore returned to Genesis and reminded myself that two distinct streams of humanity descended from Adam—one through Seth, the other through Cain—and that Enoch was the seventh from Adam *through Seth.*

Then I asked myself two questions: Who was the seventh from Adam through Cain? Were any of Cain's central characteristics reflected in his descendants? Perhaps the answers to these questions might provide a contrast to Enoch and help me understand how *not* to come to God.

Genesis 4:17–24 informs us that Lamech was the seventh man descended from Adam through Cain. He was also the first recorded polygamist in history. The way he bragged to his two wives makes it clear that he was committed to getting his own way. He said, "Wives of Lamech, hear my words. I have killed a man for wounding me, a young man for injuring me" (Gen. 4:23).

In that primitive culture, numbers meant power. Perhaps he married two wives, in disregard of God's design, to maximize his influence. The Bible does not mention Lamech's coming to God for anything, but if he ever did come to God, he probably did so to mobilize more resources for reaching his self-centered goals.

Lamech's arranging for his own well-being reflects a tendency passed down through Cain, a tendency Jude calls the "way of Cain." Included in God's punishment for killing his brother was the sentence that Cain would be "a restless wanderer on the earth" (Gen. 4:12). Cain was not permitted ever to unpack his suitcase and call any place home.*

Cain complained to God, "My punishment is more than I can bear" (Gen. 4:13). Resolved to overcome his fate, he tried to build a comfortable life for himself. He started a family and began to *build a city* (Gen. 4:17).

I must surrender my fascination with myself to a more worthy preoccupation with the character and purposes of God. I am not the point. He is. I exist for him. He does not exist for me.

Without repenting, Cain set out to overcome the consequences of his sin and to provide comfortable circumstances for himself. In effect, Cain was saying, "Okay, I'm out of the Garden. Ever since you expelled Mom and Dad from Eden and placed that angelic bouncer at the gate to keep everyone out, I realized that I must come to terms with living in a world filled with weeds and thornbushes. But even though I am out of the Garden, I will not lead the miserable life of a nomad. I will do everything I can to recapture as much of the Garden experience as possible. I will build a city, plant a few flowers, and put in a recreation park for my children. I will not keep on wandering

---

*Anyone who travels has some feel for Cain's terrible fate. My wife and I recently returned from a month-long trip in Europe in which we spent four weeks in four different countries and slept in nine different beds. During that entire trip, we never once completely unpacked our suitcases. We knew we would soon be on the move again. No place was home. Toward the end of our trip, though we were well treated by our various hosts, we both longed to return home. The first thing I did when we finally walked through our front door was to unpack my clothes and return the suitcase to its place in the basement closet. To always wander and never return home would violate something deep within me.

about without trying to settle down. I have no higher priority than arranging for my own comfort."

Because Cain passed on this attitude to his descendants, we are now able to contrast two ways of approaching life: Lamech's (reflecting the ungodly influence of Cain) and Enoch's (consistent with the godly line of Seth). Lamech declared: "I will build my city! I want my pleasures now." Enoch said: "I will build God's kingdom! And trust God to one day build a city for me to enjoy."

Because God cares deeply about his children, many times he chooses to relieve our suffering and solve our problems. But because his love is an intelligent love rooted in what he knows is best for us, he provides us with something more interesting to live for than ourselves. He catches us up in the supernatural reality of living for an eternal kingdom.

---

*The question we need to ask is this:
Are we merely living,
or are we walking with God?*

As we explore our own lives, we must never get so immersed in ourselves that we fail to remember that there is something far more wonderful to ponder. If I am to reject Lamech's approach and come to God as Enoch came, I must surrender my fascination with myself to a more worthy preoccupation with the character and purposes of God. I am not the point. He is. I exist for him. He does not exist for me.

The question we need to ask is this: Are we merely living, or are we walking with God? Are we merely committed to feeding our own souls, to arranging our lives around getting our needs met, to building our cities? Or are we committed to knowing God, to cooperating with him as loved participants in a plan larger than ourselves, to becoming like the Son whom the Father adores, and to waiting for the city that Christ is building right now?

We must learn what it means to come to God, believing that he is good when life doesn't show it, knowing that he graciously rewards honest seekers even when their souls ache relentlessly.

But can we put the lessons of Hebrew 11 more practically? What would our lives look like if we were coming to God as Enoch did?

3
Natural Passions

We all know what it means to be moved by strong, mysteriously compelling forces that emerge from somewhere deep within us. That's passion.

For some, the most driving passion occurs at the dinner table, when the urge to overeat (or undereat) irrationally consumes them. For others, their passions to buy and possess are aroused at the mall, where stores display every conceivable material fantasy.

For still others, the most powerful passion surfaces in the lonely privacy of a hotel room, where the simple push of a button fills the television screen with magnetically appealing indecency. More than a few pastors have told me of sexually explicit thoughts and feelings that rage through them as they sit on the platform Sunday mornings, waiting to preach.

For still other Christian leaders, the desire for success is the strongest passion. Jealous feelings, triggered by news of another's success, sometimes deepen an obsession to "make it big" that thoroughly corrupts a pastor's ministry.

A discussion of passion prompts a growing number of

people to reflect on their emotional battle against self-hatred. The passions of guilt and fear are the strongest emotions they feel. For others, anger is the strongest passion. Husbands feel rage every time they open the family checkbook and see the record of yet another check made out to "Cash." Wives silently boil as they listen to their husbands chat with dinner companions about their professional success, choking off any meaningful conversation about family burdens.

Still other folks report that they feel no passion. They may be effective Christian leaders whose philosophy is to get on with life no matter what happens, or driven business people who put in sixty hours every week. Or they may be frustrated singles who can't figure out how to be alive as sexual beings and, at the same time, wholesomely nonseductive.

People who feel no deep passion have only buried it. They seal their desires beneath an impenetrable wrapping that keeps them from ever being touched. They may display a glib geniality, full of good humor and warm chatter, or they may present themselves as flat and colorless, entirely unengaged with anything that would provoke strong feelings.

But, in reality, they're neither flat nor colorless. No one is. Everyone is passionately engaged in the pursuit of something. We may not feel the energy within us any more than we feel the earth rotating beneath our feet, but it's there, affecting our lives. And it's been there ever since Adam and Eve were expelled from paradise. With fierce determination, we're all searching for a plot of land with fewer weeds and thornbushes.

CITIZENS OF THIS WORLD

Without a radical shift in thinking, no one ever gives up his or her claim on land here in favor of a heavenly mansion. Our most natural passion is to make life outside the Garden of Eden a little more like we imagine it would be inside. We are more committed to making life work now than we are to finding

God and living for a later hope. We naturally turn to God only to use him to improve our present lives.

All our troublesome passions spring from this core passion to make our present lives better: distorted appetites for food or sex, bizarre urges that overwhelm us at the least convenient times, consuming desires to like ourselves better, a frantic determination to succeed personally or professionally, an insistence that spiritual victory translate into a comfortable life that no tragedy or tension can disrupt, a lust for revenge against those who have hurt us. We are passionately determined to make our lives less painful, and we will do whatever it takes to reach this goal in a disappointing, sometimes pleasurable, and maddeningly uncertain world.

We are more committed to making life work now than we are to finding God and living for a later hope. We turn to God only to use him to improve our present lives.

To feel a deep, throbbing passion about our well-being in this world is as natural as breathing. And nothing is wrong with that, *unless we feel no deeper passion!* God has told us to love him with a passion that exceeds all other passions. Until we're chasing after God like a thirsty deer after water, pursuing him with more passion than we pursue a new home, parental approval, or kids who make us proud, this world fits us well. We're conformed to its values. Our citizenship is here.

Citizens of this world live with two objectives: (1) to find some way to make their present lives happier, and (2) to influence the people and materials in their world to cooperate. Beneath their every act of altruism, benevolence, and sacrifice lies the motive of self-service that destroys its moral value.

Christians, however, are citizens of another world; in this one we are strangers, aliens, and pilgrims. Our distinguishing mark is our passion for God. We endure hardship to serve him because we love him and are confident of his promise to bless us. At least that's the plan. But our natural passions keep getting in the way. Although we claim citizenship in heaven, we live like locals.

We Christians cannot talk about loving God until we come to grips with our raging passion for ourselves. We can not and will not love anyone but ourselves until we meet God in a way that stirs us to race after him with single-minded intensity, until our deepest desire is to get to know him better.

And that's our problem. In a culture so thoroughly devoted to life now, and in a church drenched with teaching on self-improvement and building happier lives, we can't easily develop a passion for something other than our immediate satisfaction. The historic church, in its role as embassy of a foreign kingdom, taught that the chief end of people is to glorify God and enjoy him forever; the modern church too often teaches that the chief end of God is to gratify people.

We must return to our earlier understanding that personal fulfillment is not the highest value, that the well-being of any individual matters less than the glory of God, and that we will find ourselves only when we look for God first.

The historic church taught that the chief end of people is to glorify God and enjoy him forever; the modern church too often teaches that the chief end of God is to gratify people.

Is it really possible to think like that? Does anyone really sacrifice immediate well-being for the privilege of knowing Christ? Hebrews 11 is full of the stories of people—some remarkable, some ordinary, all weak and sinful—whose lives were marked by a transcendent passion for what this world could never offer. Abraham left a familiar and comfortable lifestyle to go where a supernatural voice directed him. Moses discarded the luxuries of palace living to wander through the wilderness with a million or so fickle followers. Others chose to be sawed in half rather than give up their loyalty to God.

Why? What passion drove them to forfeit their immediate comfort? Not one of them received what he naturally desired. They all died with nothing more than confidence in a God they had come to know. They were people like you and me, normal people who preferred comfort to pain—*unless comfort interfered with their finding God*. For them, nothing mattered more than finding God.

The question then is this: how can we, living centuries later in the same world full of pleasures and disappointments, with the same inclination to look after ourselves, experience that passion for God? What can we do to stir up a drive for knowing Christ that is more powerful than our natural urge to look after ourselves? How can we develop a passion for finding God that will lead to an actual encounter with him, an encounter that will free us to care about others, not to prove our value or to gain their approval, but to bless them?

That is the question I now want to address, first by asking how natural passions develop, and then, in the next chapter, by contrasting that process with the development of supernatural passions.

HOW NATURAL PASSIONS DEVELOP

Every child contends with two forces in his life: forces within himself and forces in his immediate world. From birth on, desire stirs within the *self* of the emerging person, demanding attention. Babies feel this internal passion more keenly than anything else. They naturally try to maximize pleasure and minimize pain. They want their needs satisfied.

But the *world* outside does not always cooperate. Milk doesn't always arrive on demand. Mothers sometimes seem cruelly insensitive to the desire boiling inside the self. As children grow older, other powerful forces interfere with the gratification of their desires: prettier sisters, more athletic brothers, alcoholic fathers, smothering mothers, better-dressed schoolmates, abusive uncles, mean-spirited schoolteachers, demeaning coaches, or impatient music instructors. The forces arrayed against them are everywhere! Children therefore learn rather quickly that they must protect themselves against the unpredictable forces in their world.

Typically, parents send one of two messages to their children: "We want you to be happy" or "We want you to be good."

The *self*, full of urges, longings, and dreams for its own welfare, must come to terms with a *world* full of expectations, rules, and pressures opposed to the self's agenda. How children resolve the tension between the desires of self and the demands of the world depends in part on how the parents carry out their role as the primary world for their children. Typically, parents send one of two messages to their children: "We want you to be happy" or "We want you to be good." Certainly most parents want their children to be both happy and good, but one or the other message comes across more loudly.

When parents place a premium on their children's happiness (and regard affirmation and advantages as the most important provisions the world can give to insure happiness), children are strengthened in their inclination to value *self* more than others. The world exists for them. Satisfaction of desires within them, to which they become increasingly sensitive, becomes their final value. They then set out on a lifelong mission of deciding how most effectively to use their world to realize their goal of personal comfort and joy.

When parents say, "We want you to be good,"* the tension between self and world immediately escalates. Some children relieve the tension by abandoning the self and angrily numbing its desires: "It doesn't matter who I am or how I feel. When I pay attention to my desires, I get in trouble and feel bad, so I'll ignore them. I'll do whatever is asked of me by a world more powerful than myself." (This attitude feeds contempt for oneself, not godly humility.)

Others raised in a "We-want-you-to-be-good" home handle the tension between internal desires and external demands by snubbing the world of rules and boundaries for the sake of self-preservation. They adopt an attitude that says: "I must take care of me. I'm no good to anyone else until I like me. My world is not terribly interested in helping me like myself, so I'll take on the job."

INDULGERS AND CONFORMISTS

These various styles of interacting with our world form one of two deep passions within us: *indulgence* or *conformity*. Either we look after ourselves with a blatant sense of justified self-interest, or we work hard to keep everyone in our world happy with us in order to prevent criticism, abuse, or abandonment. And these passions shape our theology.

Indulgers focus on God as little more than a predictable supplier of all their needs. He becomes the perfect world the self requires in which to develop. Indulgers learn to worship him for no higher reason than that he is committed to them. His grace becomes license for "Christianized" self-absorption: "If God loves me so much that he sent his Son to die for me, I must be

---

*This second message, "We want you to be good," often arises out of a conscious, commendable commitment by parents to mold children into responsible human beings; but it sometimes includes a definition of good that means "You must never be a nuisance to anyone, especially your parents." Neglect, abandonment, and harsh punishment forcefully teach children not to interfere with parental comfort. In these families, "Be good," means "Don't be a bother," which in turn means "Don't exist in any form we don't like."

of inestimable worth. It is right, therefore, that I devote my deepest energy to valuing myself as he does. There is no greater evil than low self-esteem."

Conformists prefer a more structured, aloof understanding of Christianity, with doctrinal precision and rule-keeping at its core. Conformists work hard to cure the moral disease of license with the deadly virus of legalism. In their particular strain of legalism, keeping rules is an end in itself, more satisfying than finding and relating to God. Their proud commitment to truth enforces the kind of obedience that never builds good relationships.

Neither indulgers nor conformists have a passion to know someone or something bigger than themselves. Nor do their lives have any purpose higher than self-preservation.

If your deepest passion is to protect yourself from a demanding world by conforming to it, the best way to get along in life is to smother the self's spark of desire under the heavy blanket of cooperation with the world, and then to parade cooperation as religious virtue. Conformists sound something like this: "Who I am doesn't really matter. Healing my childhood wounds isn't as important as following the rules. Obedience will heal whatever needs healing. I must therefore believe what is true and act accordingly. I must do right no matter how I feel. Then I'll be fine."

Although they loudly claim to be God-centered, conformists are every bit as self-oriented as indulgers. Conformists have decided that the best way to live their lives is to disregard the desires of the self and to cooperate with the world outside them. But they make this choice *to protect themselves from being destroyed by an insensitive world.* Their choice is no less self-oriented than the choice to live for self-development.

THE DEVELOPMENT OF
NATURAL PASSION

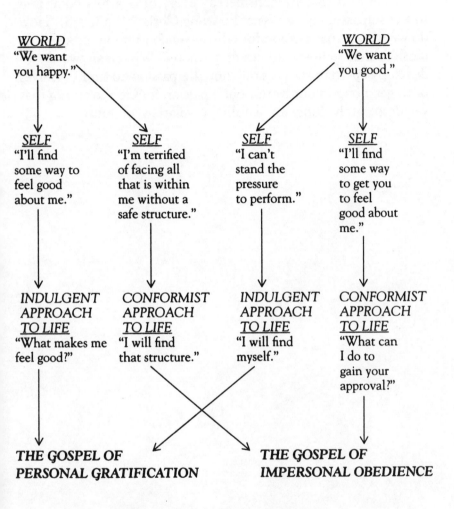

WORLD
"We want
you happy."

WORLD
"We want
you good."

SELF
"I'll find
some way to
feel good
about me."

SELF
"I'm terrified
of facing all
that is within
me without a
safe structure."

SELF
"I can't
stand the
pressure
to perform."

SELF
"I'll find
some way
to get you
to feel
good about
me."

_INDULGENT
APPROACH
TO LIFE_
"What makes me
feel good?"

_CONFORMIST
APPROACH
TO LIFE_
"I will find
that structure."

_INDULGENT
APPROACH
TO LIFE_
"I will find
myself."

_CONFORMIST
APPROACH
TO LIFE_
"What can
I do to
gain your
approval?"

_THE GOSPEL OF
PERSONAL GRATIFICATION_

_THE GOSPEL OF
IMPERSONAL OBEDIENCE_

Neither indulgers nor conformists have a passion to know someone or something bigger than themselves. Nor do their lives have any purpose higher than self-preservation. The diagram above illustrates what I've been talking about.

How do we break out of a self-oriented approach to life, an approach guided by either indulgence or conformity, and develop a transcendent passion for finding, knowing, and enjoying God?

Paul said that he considered "everything a loss compared to the surpassing greatness of knowing Christ" (Phil. 3:8). How do we stir up that passion for Christ—a consuming, controlling passion that eclipses all lesser passions? What can we do to develop supernatural passion, not the passion to find ourselves or to get along in our world, but a passion for God so strong that we desperately long for a fuller revelation of him?

4
Supernatural Passion

We cannot generate true passion for God by an act of will. No formulas will produce the passion we're after. Seasons of fasting, regular time in the Word, disciplined resistance to temptation, generous giving, exuberant worship—these are all good things, but they are not enough to fill us with passion for Christ.

True passion for our Lord is a work of the Holy Spirit. It is he who entices us, luring us to pay attention to Christ. He uncovers the stirring reality of Christ all through the Bible. Gently but firmly, he rebukes us when we dig our own wells, when we refuse Christ's invitation to come to him for living water. He gives us power to refuse fast food that tastes good but lacks nourishment. Instead, he persuades us to delight our souls in the richest of fare.

Not many of us know the powerful work of God's Spirit because, even though God draws us into loving relationship with him, we need to cooperate. We need to plow up the crusty soil of our hearts to receive the Spirit's seed. And that task is not easy.

God's Spirit gives us a fuller experience of Christ to the degree that we are willing to face terrifying truths about ourselves and life, truths that will either destroy us or drive us to trust in the Lord. To every Christian, the Holy Spirit reveals just enough about God to support the next level of personal honesty.

If we choose to face the difficult realities the Holy Spirit enables us to face, he then grants a fuller vision of God that permits the process to continue. If we turn from those realities, refusing to believe that God can keep us intact no matter what pain we feel, the Spirit is quenched. He reveals no more of God to us.

Part of our job then, if we are to find God, is to look honestly at those disturbing realities about ourselves and life—realities that could destroy all our joy unless God gives us hope.

The Spirit will focus our blurred vision of God as we pursue an *awareness* of ourselves that *immobilizes* us into a state of spiritual *alertness*, in which we are eager to hear the voice of God.

Let me briefly define the key words in this sentence before discussing them more extensively:

Awareness: the growing realization of what really is happening in us and in our relationships based on a determination to pretend about nothing.

Immobility: an internal stillness, a loss of energy that comes from realizing that no amount of effort on our part will help us recover the bliss of Eden.

Alertness: a tingling anticipation of God's revealing himself to us.

AWARENESS

Maturing Christians are *aware*. They face life as it really is, pretending about nothing. They are drawn more to knowing Christ than to enjoying their own worth. They are caught up with the beauty of Christ in a way that frees them from coveting opportunities to "express" themselves. They cling to their hope in Christ during those dark days when it seems easier to deaden themselves than to suffer one more assault from life.

We all *fear* that life is intolerable and overwhelming, but we don't want to *admit* it. To do so would require a terrifying dependence on God. But the fabric of life *is* shredded beyond repair. Legislation, therapy, social action, church programs, personal growth seminars—nothing can sew it back together. When we realize that we can't fully mend the fabric of life, we first feel discouraged and defeated, a feeling that may last a long time. But eventually the Spirit of God compels us to move back into the world, with needle and thread in hand, to repair what we can until the Master Tailor returns and crafts a new heaven and a new earth.

We will never fully mend the rip—only God can accomplish that. But we have a larger purpose than patching up life: to know God and enjoy him forever.

How can we become more *aware* of what we tend to deny and thereby know God more intimately? The more aware we become of certain truths about what life is really like, the more committed we will be to knowing God, and the less concerned we will be about solving our immediate problems.

Let me list five truths that I am facing more fully as I pursue God. You cannot learn these truths merely by reading about them. You can learn them only through experiencing them. As you face your life honestly, perhaps God will use these truths to draw you more fully to himself.

Our deepest longings are inconsolable.

C. S. Lewis once said: "If I find in myself a desire which no experience in this world can satisfy, the most probable explanation is that I was made for another world."

Still, I find myself clinging to this world and to the legitimate joys it affords. My mind is flooded with memories of playing tennis: my brother, Bill, serving to Dad's backhand, me at the net hoping to get my racket on the return. When the game was over, we'd return home to Mother's special blend of iced tea. It was the four of us then.

Later, it was another four: our two sons, Kep and Ken, my wife, Rachael, and I. Trips to the Grand Canyon, to the Florida Keys with Rachael's parents, to a mission base in Columbia, South America; times together eating pizza or chicken crescents (a "Rachael specialty"), watching Wimbledon on a big-screen TV, or meeting at the table to discuss family tensions.

Both our boys are now men, living on their own. Rachael and I enjoy a full life together. Our bond has never been stronger. But sometimes we ache for what has passed. Her parents are both in their eighties. Both she and I have lost brothers in airplane crashes—her brother died more than twenty-five years ago. But the pain of his loss does not go away.

The deepest pleasures of life don't satisfy—they point us forward.

Things have changed. And even though I rejoice in the blessings of my life as it is now, I mourn the passing of the years, the changes in my family, the loss of brothers to death. I want what this life cannot provide. I want rich, legitimate pleasures that never end.

We should appreciate and enjoy all the good things in this life, because they are given by a God "who richly provides us with everything for our enjoyment" (1 Tim. 6:17). But these good things are no more than appetizers. The real meal is yet to come. And the closest we can come now to enjoying that meal is to develop a taste for intimacy with Christ. Nothing less will delight our souls "with the richest of fare" (Isa. 55:2).

Most of us, however, keep trying to make a meal out of the appetizers, then complain when we are not filled. We think that we should be satisfied if we marry the right person, or if we excel at and enjoy our work, or if we are wealthy enough to buy whatever we desire. But these things are only appetizers. Why do our taste buds react more positively to good things than to the best? Why must we *acquire* a taste for Christ?

We all sense that we are hungry for something more than the appetizers of life, but we work hard to avoid that realization. Either we deaden our deepest hunger with activity, platitudes, and pleasures, or we think about the dark side of life so much that we feel we have things under control: Each new insight into the awful complexity of living, each new awareness of how badly we've suffered, encourages the false hope that awareness of pain will somehow enable us to triumph nobly over it. But still the hunger remains. And to develop an awareness of God, we have to face that hunger head on and recognize both its source and its fulfillment. We have to acknowledge that our hunger for God comes from him and will not be completely satisfied on this earth. The deepest pleasures of life don't satisfy—they point us forward. Until we attain unity with Christ in heaven, an inconsolable longing for *more* will remain in every human heart.

Other people's lives testify to the value of knowing God better.

A second important truth is that a few choice saints testify to the possibility of knowing God better. They stand out in the crowd, not because they do more, or seem more blessed with talent and effectiveness in ministry, but simply because they are better people.

We are drawn to them not merely because of their moral superiority or their richer capacity to love, but because of the strong impression that these folks know God in a way we don't.

Scripture records stories of ordinary people—weak, stumbling, sinful people—who found a path to God and stayed on it. Hosea proclaimed God's compassion even though his own heart was shattered by an unfaithful wife. Habakkuk skipped through mountains while trembling with terror over his country's imminent destruction. The hatred of friends couldn't drown God's fire in Jeremiah's heart. And Peter was so thrilled with the memory of Christ's sacrifice he didn't feel worthy to die in the same upright position as his Lord. He requested his executioner to crucify him upside down.

But we don't have to go back to biblical times to find people worthy of notice. Most of us have stumbled across the path of someone who provokes in us an uncomfortable sense of feeling small and behind schedule, someone who talks about Christ with the warm familiarity of intimate friendship, someone who has endured loneliness and heartbreak with uncomplaining sadness, accepting pain as a difficult privilege that opens the door to richer closeness with Christ. Some, of course, speak with a richness that is more show than substance, and they provoke in others pressure and guilt rather than a thirst to know God. But the few who truly know God entice us to sacrifice whatever we must in order to gain their knowledge.

Most of these people are older and reluctant to talk about themselves. They're easy to pass by. We tend to dismiss them as too old and out of touch, not aware of the psychological struggles of modern life, stuck in a narrow theology that gives insufficient room for the human spirit to breathe and stretch, too preoccupied with ideas that don't apply to life on the street.

But we should listen to these men and women whose passion for God has loosened their attachment to everything here on earth. Exposure to people like this creates a holy covetousness, a desperate desire to know God better.

We are inescapably selfish.

A third important truth is that we are inescapably selfish. We put ourselves and our own well-being first. Then, to make things worse, we don't even recognize how self-centered we really are.

Our culture encourages this self-centeredness. It is consumed with healing the pain of our underdeveloped, restricted, shame-filled, brutalized selves. Modern thinking encourages us to find ourselves, to heal our shame, and to pursue self-fulfillment. And as a consequence, we value healing for our pain more than pardon for our sin; we view God's kindness as more appropriate than surprising, more immediately helpful than deeply humbling.

A good friend of mine is married to an extremely difficult woman. She is cold, critical, and mean-spirited. The first woman in his life was no better. His mother was—and still is—an angry alcoholic. He was raised in an atmosphere of severe emotional abuse.

We value healing for our pain more than pardon for our sin.

My friend is in pain not of his own making. Whatever responsibility he bears for his choice of a mate or perhaps for ineffectively handling his mother and wife, he is still a victim. He bears the wounds of others' sin.

Without question, this man needs encouragement. He needs to know that the shameful treatment he has endured is no measure of his worth. He needs to set boundaries between himself and his abusers by doing such things as refusing to talk to his mother when she criticizes him and drags him down.

But the path to joy lies not in recovery from his wounds or in setting boundaries, but in identifying and repenting of his commitment to advance his own well-being as he sees fit. When that commitment takes priority over his determination to know God and make him known to others, then my friend is wrong. His worst problem is sin, not pain.

We need to see ourselves as more sinful than wounded. We need to face the ugly, self-centered energy present in all our conversations. As we become more aware of our self-centeredness, our demand to feel better weakens under our developing humility. Awareness of our self-centeredness puts us in touch with our longing for a clean heart and a giving spirit. Awareness of God's forgiveness makes us gratefully amazed that we are accepted by someone who sees us at our worst.

When we're properly stunned as we sing "Amazing Grace," the focus shifts *away from* our struggle to find our identity and *toward* a fascination with the character of Someone who could actually love people who spit on him. And then, with our focus on Christ where it belongs, personal identity gradually falls into place.

The Holy Spirit is a person who works in our lives.

The Holy Spirit is neither an impersonal force to be used, like electricity, nor a divine bubble machine that transforms dreary lives into an exciting party. Rather, the Holy Spirit is a *person* who works in our lives. He is a *person* every bit as real as our spouses and kids, but a supernatural person who haunts our lives with a strange presence that seems eerie only because, in our dullness, the world we can see seems more real than the one he inhabits.

We are given to excesses in opposite directions. Either we shy away from the supernatural, or we expect its manifestation on demand. Perhaps the balance lies in an eager openness to the Spirit's movement, an anticipation of his presence that listens for the sound of blowing wind but never shakes the tree to get the leaves moving.

God is always up to something. Our job is to remain sensitive to whatever that may be. We can be sure of this: when the Spirit blows, terrifying disruption and seductive enticement will be felt. Old foundations will crumble, and we will fall to greater heights. His delight is to lift us to another dimension that feels both eerily strange and warmly familiar.

It is difficult to enter a reality that we can't see. But when the Spirit opens the door, when we catch a glimpse of the other side, we cannot stay where we've been.

We are given to excesses in opposite directions. Either we shy away from the supernatural, or we expect its manifestation on demand.

As we reflect more on the Spirit's haunting presence, his single-minded purpose of promoting Christ, and his transcendent power to keep us going, perhaps we'll realize how arrogant it is of us either to ignore him or try to figure him out. And we'll become more aware of how badly we want him to do his work in our lives.

Suffering is inevitable.

A final important truth is that suffering is inevitable. Proud people want an explanation of whatever goes wrong. If we discover that our fear of intimacy is a result of childhood abuse, then our lives seem more under control. Now we have something to work on to make things better. By thinking hard about the human condition and coming up with theories about what is going on, we destroy mystery, and we maintain the illusion that, with enough insight and effort, we can take care of ourselves and our suffering will end.

A trip to a third-world country, where people live with a definition of comfort unimaginably different from ours, may realign our perspective with an eternal one. It is good to relieve suffering wherever we can and to promote personal recovery and physical comfort, but something else matters more.

There is more to life than recovering from hardship. Neither our personal pain nor the struggles of millions to survive can serve as the organizing focus of life. *Future hope is more valuable than present relief.* Until we realize this, we are not on the path to finding God.

IMMOBILITY

Despite our best efforts, life never gets quite good enough. Our standards are never met. Even the happiest lives have pockets of incurable pain. When we face that fact, something important happens. The determination to make life work loses steam; we slow down and become open to changing direction.

When we become aware of our incurable pain, we will cry out to God in rage and sorrow. "Cure our pain!" we plead. "Deliver us from our enemies!" But God does not reliably respond as we wish, and finally we slump, exhausted, robbed of the energy we need to focus on relieving our own problems.

As exhaustion immobilizes us, as we lose interst in making things better, we are slowly freed to pursue God. We are desperate now not for solutions *from* God, but for fellowship *with* God. Awareness of what is true about ourselves, about life, and about God shuts us up, and makes us view with disgust and shame-filled futility our efforts to make life work. Why bother? It isn't worth it. Nothing that I do will ever provide me with what my soul yearns for the most.

We then find ourselves reduced to motionless inactivity, standing still, naked before God. Powerless to improve our own lives, we crouch before God filled with fear and dread because he has refused to be controlled by us. Instead, he commands us: "Be still, and know that I am God" (Ps. 46:10).

With a pain beyond tears, the kind of pain only still people know, we feel how bad we want to taste Christ, how desperately we long for God to let us find him. And with longing beyond words, we groan with the intensity of our desire to know him, now lying on the ground face down, prostrate beneath the cold sky, afraid to look up, one moment hoping that God will leave us alone in our misery rather than destroy us with his presence, and the next hoping against hope that he will reveal a heart of merciful love. The moments pass, sometimes years. And we lie still.

More than once I have risen from bed at 2 A.M., unable to

lie still because of anger-filled and terrifying thoughts. It often begins innocently, perhaps with the realization of a tax deadline or an unprepared lecture I must give next Wednesday.

Then, like one billiard ball striking another, that one thought triggers others: phone calls to make, tensions to handle, mail to answer, difficult decisions that no longer can be avoided. I break out in a cold sweat. A strange dread descends that seems to have its source in more than the responsibilities I must face. Life seems too big for me. I am not up to its demands.

I feel furious at whoever requires something of me. Why won't someone understand and give me a break? With fuming resignation, I admit no one will, not even God. He won't do my tax return for me.

So I scramble to recover. I plot my strategy. Tomorrow I'll gather last year's receipts, then I'll outline my lecture after the three appointments I regret having scheduled. Maybe I'll cancel them. No, that wouldn't be responsible. But I'm pressed for time. They'll just have to understand.

One morning several months ago, after tossing about with thoughts like these, I stood at the foot of my bed, unable to move for perhaps ten minutes. Finally a leg cramp moved me back to bed. I stayed there for an hour, unable to sleep. "God, where are you? What are you supposed to be doing? Can't you see I'm desperate? *What good are you?*"

I heard no answer. Eventually, from sheer exhaustion, I fell asleep, immobilized, wanting with all my heart to hear from God.

ALERTNESS

As we remain prostrate, without scrambling for a way to revive our spirits enough to stand up and carry on with life, we hear a new voice, faint at first, but clearer and more real than any we've ever before heard. It calls us to pray, to feed on God's Word, to imagine that our wildest dreams will soon be reality.

That morning a few months ago brought something close to revival. I awoke from my troubled sleep, still feeling immobilized. I had no energy. Like a puppet pulled by strings, I managed to crawl out of bed and stumble into the shower stall.

I knew one thing. Without a deeper revelation of God, I would have no energy and no reason to do anything. I was trapped by him.

And then, as I showered, the thought struck me: others go through trials similar to mine, some far worse. Many have already endured and remained faithful. Others have much ahead to face. Perhaps, I thought, I can draw strength from those ahead of me and become a source of strength for those still behind.

I remember smiling at that point. If that's true, I thought, then there's reason to sing. So, with respect for a great tradition, I burst into song while hot water pounded on my back. God had spoken to me. I had been immobilized by terror into a state of alertness that allowed me to hear God's voice.

That's how it sometimes happens. We begin to *sense* a truth that we formerly could only *explain*, that God does *not* despise a broken and contrite spirit. Without noticing the movement, certainly without conscious effort, we rise to our feet, slowly, somehow beckoned and then irresistibly empowered to do so, and we become alert to a dimension of living that feels strangely familiar. A sense of impending reunion with someone we've never met but have always known makes us tingle with unendurably passionate anticipation.

For a few moments, we became alive with a consuming passion to know Christ, to taste him as we would a nourishing meal, and to enjoy him as a cherished bride enjoys the wedding night with her bridegroom.

Our prayer life is changed. Now we actually talk with someone we know as a Father in the very best sense of that word. We read the Bible with new delight. Statements we heard as children about the Bible being a love letter finally begin to make sense. Our hearts burn within us because we see

Christ in every story and epistle. We know the Holy Spirit in new ways that feel personal and unmistakably present, and we sense the loving, mighty hand of God on our lives and in our hearts.

Then, as it always does, the glow fades. We look around us and realize we're still out of the Garden. The car breaks down, and we call the people with the tow truck, who arrive two hours late and overcharge us for their services. A plane crashes, and we mourn the death of a husband, father, son, brother, friend. Our bodies grow weary more quickly, and new aches and pains appear almost daily. Gas tanks run empty. Power companies want to be paid. Depression recurs. Sexual struggles that seemed to disappear come back.

Employers ignore good performance, and hard work goes unrewarded. Someone snubs us and we're flooded with self-hatred. A good friend gets caught in an affair. An unmarried daughter tells her parents she's pregnant, and a son is arrested for drug possession.

Was that moment of knowing God real? Was it fantasy? Is he really there? Do I want to know him, or do I just want a way out, a way to feel better? Is there any joy in Christ *apart* from the blessings of godly kids, good friends, health, and money? Could I make it with *just him?*

And then our attention returns, in no particular order, to that inconsolable longing, the enticement of godly people, our wretched self-centeredness, the reality of God's Spirit, the inevitability of suffering, and our hope for a better day—and again we're immobilized. The frantic pressure to handle everything is relieved, and we fall down, stilled by the overwhelming awareness of our souls, life, and the eternal: reduced to wanting God—and nothing more. The tingle of anticipation returns, and we realize that the hope within us has not died. Then he speaks. Once again, our hearts are lifted along with our bodies, and we sing, we dance, we shout for joy.

Then life continues. Another day, another disappointment, another pleasure. But now, as we walk along the path of everyday living, something is different. Our focus is drawn more easily to Christ. And slowly we change. Some even report a glow, an enticing fragrance.

Is there any joy in Christ apart from the blessings of godly kids, good friends, health, and money? Could I make it with just him?

Then one day we move from this world to the next. And our Lord greets us with a bear hug. We collapse before him in reverence and wonder, but his embrace keeps us close. He laughs and says, "Look behind you!" And there is our brother who died years ago, happier than we've ever seen him, and our parents, and our miscarried baby, and Dr. Luke, and Elijah, and Enoch. Now *we're* laughing. We can't stop. And the sweetest voice in all creation says, "Welcome. You're finally home!"

But we have a long way to go before we get there. Our spiritual journey has barely begun.

II
THE OBSTACLE TO
FINDING GOD

5
Something Is
Seriously Wrong

I n the months following the plane crash that took my brother's life, I repeatedly asked God to use Bill's death to change me into the mature man I long to be. I didn't want the pain to be wasted. Believing that the horror of what happened could be turned to good made it more bearable. The accident introduced me to a new level of suffering; I wanted the suffering to lift me to a new level of maturity.

Perhaps I was asking for more. I have a hard time living in a capricious world. I like things to make sense, to be well-ordered by someone who knows what he's doing. I don't like chaos. If my maturity shot up dramatically after Bill's death, I might more easily accept the tragedy as the hard part of a good plan. Whatever the reasons for my prayer, I knew one thing as I prayed: I wanted to find a way that led through my heartache to God. And when I found him, I wanted him to make me a better man and my world a little less maddening.

Notice the purpose driving my search for God: finding him had more to do with *using* him to get what I valued (a better me and a less maddening world) than *enjoying* him for who he is. I wanted to harness his power rather than submit to it.

STILL A MESS

As I reflect on my life today, nearly a year after the crash, I conclude that my prayer for maturity has not been answered as I had wished, no more than my prayer for the safety of family members was answered on that terrible day in March. In spite of passionate pleas for maturity, I'm still a mess. If I have a new glow about me, I rarely see it. And when I do think I catch a glimpse, it quickly fades.

I'm still far too irritable. The slightest provocation can send a wave of fury through me that delights in destroying whatever lies in its path. At times, I'm as thin-skinned as a spoiled child. If my wife, Rachael, criticizes something I do or fails to respond to my moods supportively, a pettiness, both deliciously powerful and repulsively immature, sometimes rises within me. Have I changed? I reacted the same way a quarter of a century ago when we first married.

Notice the purpose driving my search for God: finding him had more to do with using him to get what I valued than enjoying him for who he is. I wanted to harness his power rather than submit to it.

Unholy desires still burn within me. Middle age is not refining my appetites. Other feelings—some good, some bad—come and go, seemingly at their own whim. For no reason, I sometimes plummet into a loneliness that swallows every trace of joy and weakens my usual passion for people and things.

For years, I have lived through seasons of self-hatred when I feel unwanted and unwantable. This self-loathing feels like a poisoned apple: Observe me from a distance and you may think me desirable. Get close enough to handle me and still I look good. Bite into me and you'll be harmed, perhaps destroyed.

These poisonous feelings severely distort my thinking, drain me of productive energy, and shut me up in the perverse joys of sulking.

I sometimes lose the vision for what God wants to do through my life. When that happens, I either panic or feel lifelessly indifferent. When I panic, I accept too many opportunities for ministry, preferring the possibility of burnout to the risk of being shelved. When apathy sets in, I feel put upon by people who want to exploit my gifts but care nothing for me.

Am I improving? Or getting worse? Has my fervent pursuit of God moved me along the path that leads to enjoyable fellowship with Christ? Or am I on the wrong path? Or am I standing still?

Finding God in this life does not mean building a house in a land of no storms; rather it means building a house that no storm can destroy.

People who know me would say that I am painting an unfairly harsh picture of myself. And, happily, I agree. All that I've said is true, but I'm not telling the whole story. I gratefully acknowledge that I am a generous person, often thoughtful, sometimes sacrificially kind. I work hard. I am deeply committed to my family. I am serious about my faith. I am neither dishonest on my tax forms nor immoral in motel rooms. I have made an impact on others' lives. I know more of God now than I ever have before.

But honest scrutiny of my life still reveals much lacking. I long to be what I am not, to feel what I rarely feel, to love as I have never loved. Too often, I feel weak, empty, frenzied, lonely, preoccupied, angry, and jealous. Can these feelings coexist with maturity, or are they proof of its opposite?

One thing is clear. By the standards of perfect humanity,

embodied fully only in Jesus Christ, each of us has much farther to go than we have already gone. The elimination of struggle and the ability to love someone else perfectly describe our lives in heaven, not maturity on this earth. No matter how well I come to know the Lord, until I actually see him, my life will still be a mess—and so will yours. Finding God in this life does not mean building a house in a land of no storms; rather it means building a house that no storm can destroy.

Am I building that house? Are you? Are we moving through our problems toward finding God? Do we know what it means to dig deeply enough to discover something other than more problems—to discover Someone beyond ourselves? Have we hit rock?

A NODDING ACQUAINTANCE WITH GOD

It has been nearly two years since I prayed, "Lord, I know you're all I have, but I don't know you well enough for you to be all I need. Please let me find you." In that time it has become more clear to me that neither spiritual discipline nor self-exploration carries me where I want to go. Confessing sins, reconciling with estranged friends, and spending regular time in the Word are all necessary and right. But the more I wrestle with life as it really is, the more I am aware that living a spiritually disciplined life develops at best only a nodding acquaintance with God.

Exploring my motives more thoroughly or rummaging through my past to dredge up connections between childhood hurts and present struggles provokes more frustration than hope. This self-examination may help me to know *myself* better, but I want to know God. My countless hours providing therapy for hundreds of people suggests that a focus on increased knowledge of self rarely leads to richer knowledge of God. Getting better acquainted with ourselves in order to find God— and doing nothing more—is like endlessly studying an X-ray of spot-riddled lungs without ever submitting to surgery.

Neither spiritual discipline nor self-understanding reliably leads where I long to go. The former too often creates a smug Pharisee; the latter, a liberated modern who cannot think beyond self-enjoyment. What am I to do? I am nearing the half-century mark still troubled by a generous supply of problems. Important parts of life, both within me and in my world, remain a mystery. I'm losing confidence in my ability to navigate the dark waters of relationship and responsibility, but more than ever I long to sail through them to the bright harbor beyond.

THE EVIL STRUCTURE WITHIN US

The more I commit myself to finding God in the middle of life's struggles, the more I become aware of something terribly wrong within me, something so evil that it must be overcome, but so strong that it reliably overcomes me. And yet it must be weakened and eventually destroyed. As long as this dark problem within me remains unchallenged, I will never find God.

But the problem is stubborn. It seems to have an organized, resilient life of its own. I, therefore, describe it as a structure within me, a fallen way of thinking about God, ourselves, and others that opposes everything true.

Think of this *fallen structure* as built on a foundation with five "floors" or levels, each building on the one beneath it.

The pyramid-like structure on the next page gives you a visual representation of the structure. The foundation of this structure, which I will describe in chapter 7, is "I Doubt God." The floors that build on this foundation are "I Need You," "I Hate You," "I Hate Me," "But I Will Survive," and finally, "Here's How I Will Survive." All the nonmedical problems clients bring to counselors, problems of life that all of us experience in varying degrees of severity, arise from this firmly entrenched structure.

Our inclination to sin is rooted in the suspicion that God is not all that good. Doubting God's goodness is the foundation

THE FALLEN STRUCTURE
OF THE HUMAN PERSONALITY

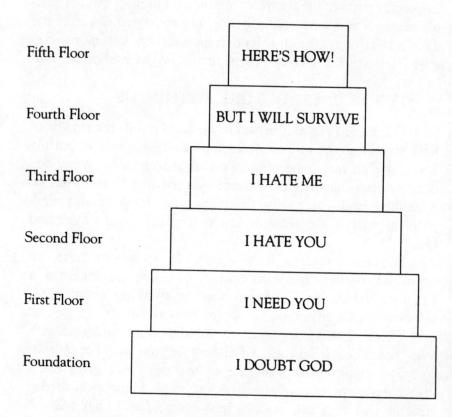

PROBLEMS IN LIVING

Fifth Floor	HERE'S HOW!
Fourth Floor	BUT I WILL SURVIVE
Third Floor	I HATE ME
Second Floor	I HATE YOU
First Floor	I NEED YOU
Foundation	I DOUBT GOD

of our fallen structure. If we believe God is powerful, we're not convinced that he is kind because, if he *can* relieve our suffering, why *doesn't* he? The silence of God during tough times strengthens this foundational doubt that God is good.

6
When God Won't Let Us Find Him

N othing is more easily taken for granted than a faith that is unchallenged. As long as things go our way, we continue with a confidence in God that seems strong and healthy. We assume that, spiritually, things are fine.

But what happens when our trust is severely challenged? What happens when life crashes down on us with shattering force? When tensions in important relationships seem utterly unresolvable? When health or job problems isolate us with no one but God—and he doesn't show up?

SUICIDE ON CHRISTMAS DAY

The phone rang as I was writing that last paragraph. I put down my pen to answer it and listened as a pastor-friend told me that his friend's twenty-four-year-old son had committed suicide last week—on Christmas day.

As I replaced the phone in its cradle, the questions came, unbidden and unexpected, rushing through me like a torrent, carrying me into uncharted regions of thought that made me feel alive with dark passion:

"God, couldn't you have made it clear to this young man's godly parents that something was dreadfully wrong? Couldn't you then have given them the wisdom to know how to restore hope to their son's troubled soul? Their pain must be unimaginable! Don't you care?

"And couldn't somebody have done something two weeks ago—or maybe ten years ago—that would have made the difference between life and death? Why didn't you lead someone to reach out to that young man? God, what's the matter with you?"

Even as I asked the questions, I knew they would not be answered. No one knows the answers—except God. And he isn't talking, at least not with the answers I demand. Some say that God gives a richer sense of his presence in the midst of confusion and grief, and he does—but not always. Sometimes he allows us to suffer alone, with no comfort beyond what he has already said in his Word. Older Christians sometimes report that definite answers to prayer were more common in their earlier years. But I still want answers—sometimes more than I want God.

THE FATHERLESS AND THE WIDOWS

My paternal grandmother lost her husband when he was only thirty years old and had to raise four children by herself. Once, handing my father a coin to buy bread, she said, "Now remember, Lawrence, this is our last nickel. Don't lose it."

I still want answers—sometimes more
than I want God.

My grandmother placed her complete confidence in the Lord, who in his Word had promised to defend "the cause of the fatherless and the widow" (Deut. 10:18). Is this how God keeps his promise? By leaving a fatherless and husbandless family at poverty level, worried lest they lose five cents!

The four fatherless children, each in their own way, also paid a hard price. Because he had to help support the family, my father never had the opportunity to challenge his excellent mind with advanced education. As a result, when he later had to provide for our family, he sold machines all day and devoured poetry and literature and Scripture at night. Is that God's version of defending the fatherless, to rob a man of legitimate avenues of fulfillment?

My widowed grandmother lost her eyesight during her last years of life. After years of struggling with poverty and loneliness, and never wavering in faith, she ended her days in literal darkness. Is this another example of God keeping his promise to "defend the cause of the widow"?

LIFE IS MADDENING

I have spent my entire adult life trying to understand people and life, wanting to know how God relates with us and how he works in our lives. And I have learned much. But some things lie far beyond the reach of human comprehension. Godly parents lose their children to drugs, suicide, or materialism. Good families are torn apart by unresolvable tensions, while strong Christians sometimes emerge from terrible homes.

Life is so maddening, so stubbornly uncooperative with our best efforts to reduce it to a straight-line, cause-and-effect flow chart. When I was a kid, I sometimes scored an A on a test the morning after I had flagrantly sinned. And sometimes I did poorly after a whole week of righteous living. It didn't make sense then, and it doesn't make sense now.

When I allow myself to think deeply about it, I realize that I can't guarantee that no one I love will ever take his or her own life. Some things I can do will lower the probabilities, but playing the odds is not terribly comforting.

If people were to balance everyday demonstrations of God's kindness against evidences of divine indifference, and then determine their level of trust by the position of the scales, very few joyfully confident, exuberantly committed Christians would be running about. Judging from what I see in the world around me, I can have no certainty that God is working in my life as I want him to any more than he worked in the life of this grieving family who lost their son on Christmas day, or in the life of my grandmother, who struggled to raise four children on her own.

UNNECESSARY PESSIMISM?

Perhaps I am painting an overly bleak picture. After all, my grandmother *did* make it through those hard years. My father saw the fruits of his love, hard work, and good mind in his two sons. And maybe God will bring some good out of the tragic suicide of this twenty-four-year-old.

But that idea doesn't always work. There are some tragedies—and I have seen them—where no clear good emerges. As far as we can see, they are senseless, random, utterly without redeeming usefulness. I have seen a woman's father die a week before she was returning home to reconcile with him. I have seen a man hear his unwed daughter announce her pregnancy the same day his son was arrested for theft. I have seen a godly woman contract a rare disease after years of patiently enduring a dead marriage. I have seen a happy young family plunged into despair when the father accidentally backed the car over his three-year-old son. In each case, God did not let his purposes for the tragedy be known.

When we are confronted with the inscrutable nature of God, when we are left without even the faintest sense of God's presence, we often respond in one of two ways.

A FOOL'S PARADISE

One response to the hiddenness of God is to *live in a fool's paradise.*

Deny how much you struggle and hurt. Ignore your unanswerable questions. Keep telling yourself that everything is all right, that you love Jesus, that you love others, and that your trust in Christ is supplying you with fast-flowing streams of living water. Never listen to honest preachers who let you know they still struggle. Attend a church where the pastor, if he shares anything personal at all, describes either problems from long ago that maturity has now resolved or current naughtiness that reveals his appealing vulnerability more than his ongoing battle with sin. Make sure his commitment is to preach the Word of God to insure doctrinal accuracy among the faithful, never to promote relational integrity or sheer passion. Avoid like the plague a community of hungry, distraught people who, in their pursuit of more, ask questions that routine exegesis cannot handle.

After hearing my teaching on this, a man named Doug was clearly offended. "I see no value to rummaging through your life to find pain," he said to me. "God tells me to forget what's behind and get on with my life. When I face a problem, I go to the Word to find out what it says. And then it is up to me whether I obey. If I do what God tells me, then he blesses; if not, he disciplines. Why do you complicate things so much with all your talk of relationship and longings and motives. You're bringing the Trojan horse of psychology into the church. Stick with the Bible. Keep it simple. Do whatever God says."

Like so many, Doug was running from the hard facts of life by insisting that Christianity offers a simple formula for making life work. Parents who obey God have good kids. Parents who disobey God have problem kids. It's that simple!

Because Doug used obedience to avoid pain, he was living in a fool's paradise.

THE COUNSELING BANDWAGON

A second way to make life work is to *join the counseling bandwagon.* Realize that the church is dangerous to your health. Learn to hate denial more than you hate anything else. Regard it as the unpardonable sin. Demand satisfying answers to every question. Figure things out. Avoid mystery. Face everything within you that hurts, and then develop a theology that zeroes in on shame and self-hatred as the problems that burden God more than all others.

Make it your top priority to become personally healthy. Keep on pressing toward a happier life, greater wholeness, and a non-shame-based identity. Disguise the ugliness of your selfish pursuit by defining your goal as spiritual maturity or Christlikeness. See to it that you stop at nothing to overcome your addictions, your low self-esteem, your codependent patterns of relating. Remember, *you* are the point—and God is there to remind you of your value and to help you solve whatever problems interfere with your personal fulfillment.

Don't give in to the nagging suspicion that many problems may not be resolved till heaven and that perhaps many were not *meant* to be resolved till then. Resist the idea that God wants to invade your heart at a level deeper than your pain and to give you reason and power to continue doing good no matter how you feel. Don't settle for postponed fulfillment. Claim it now!

Don't pay attention to those who invite you into the darkness of mystery where no plan of action sheds light, where your anguish of soul cannot be relieved by obedience but can only be absorbed in trust.

Shortly after Doug talked to me, another listener, Lisa, wanted time to share. "So much of your teaching is really helpful, but I want to tell you how I've taken it further," she said eagerly. I agreed to meet with her the next day.

When we met, she said, "Larry, I love your work, but at times you seem so negative. I just discovered a pastor who led me through healing prayer. It was nothing short of a miracle. He brought me before the cross until God's love poured over me like a bucket of warm water. All my pain just melted away. I've never been happier in my life. Isn't God wonderful?"

Because she seemed to be focusing on a plan to generate happy feelings, I asked her: "Do you suppose God might lead you through deep suffering that he wants you to endure for good reason—and may, therefore, not relieve?"

"If the pain I felt returns," she replied, "I will seek more counseling and healing prayer. I believe God wants me to enjoy my value as his child."

People who value resolution of pain over learning to love often jump onto the counseling bandwagon that offers solutions to problems rather than a pathway to God.

A THIRD OPTION

These are the two common directions of our culture. The first, common in fundamentalist circles, crushes the soul under the weight of academic truth and proud obedience. The second, popular among church renewal advocates, creates an illusion of life that honors the deadly virus of selfishness by calling it a different name. Neither addresses us as thoroughly *fallen* creatures. The first approach seems to imply that we can pick ourselves up from where we have fallen by a mere act of will. The second defines our helpless condition as morally excusable and therefore values God's help above his mercy.

But there is a third option—an approach that equips us to dive into the cesspool of the human heart, find hidden treasure, and come up laughing. This third option comes to grips with a reality that the other two either trivialize or ignore—an utterly false way of thinking about God, ourselves, and others that I call the fallen structure of the human personality. This third option requires that we face the fallen structure in all of its loathsome, stubborn, wicked power and submit to a painful process of dismantling.

7
The Foundation of the Fallen Structure: Doubting God

T o describe the fallen structure of the human personality is to paint a portrait of the fallen soul. Something inside me is desperately wrong. There is a fundamental flaw in each of us that the Bible calls by several names, including "the body of sin" (Rom. 6:6), "the sinful nature" (Gal. 5:16), and "the law of sin" (Rom. 7:23). Although distinctions can be made among these terms, each one points to the central obstacle to knowing God.

If we are to find God as he wants to be found, if we are to know him in a way that frees us to live with joy and purpose and self-control, then we must not work primarily to solve our problems; we must rather cooperate with God's work to disrupt and destroy this fallen structure.

THE TEMPTATION IN THE GARDEN

Scripture tells us that the crafty serpent tempted Eve to sin by first deceiving her. He deceived her by inviting her to question the motives behind God's prohibition. "Did God really say, 'You must not eat from any tree in the garden'?" (Gen. 3:1).

Embedded in that question is this idea: "I can't believe it! God really told you not to do that? That's like a mother telling her child not to play with a wonderful toy."

The deception worked. Apparently, Eve began to wonder if God was holding out on her. She replied, "We may eat fruit from the trees in the garden, but God did say, 'You must not eat fruit from the tree that is in the middle of the garden, and you must not touch it, or you will die'" (Gen. 3:2).

Eve was led into error on three counts. First, God had told Adam and Eve that they were "free to eat fruit from *any* tree" except one. Eve said, "We may eat fruit from the trees in the garden." She missed her freedom to enjoy God's abundant supply.

Second, the *tree of life* was in the center of the garden, perhaps along with the forbidden tree (Gen. 2:9). Eve saw only the forbidden tree. She lost sight of the truth that God's plan for his children is life, not prohibitions.

Third, she added to God's restriction when she responded that God required her not to even touch the wrong tree. When rules are emphasized more than liberty, the rules begin to multiply. The multiplication continues till we develop a code of rules so complete that we no longer enjoy our relationship with the rule-giver. The letter of the law then quenches the spirit (2 Cor. 3:6).

The serpent quickly capitalized on Eve's errors. "You will not surely die," he said. "For God knows that when you eat of it your eyes will be opened, and you will be like God, knowing good and evil" (Gen. 3:4–5).

The deception was complete, and it yielded sin. Seeing that "the fruit of the tree was good for food and pleasing to the eye, and also desirable for gaining wisdom, [Eve] took some and ate it" (Gen. 3:6). God, she concluded, was holding out on her. There was something good he didn't want her to enjoy. She couldn't deny that God had given her much that was good, but the serpent got her thinking that God was withholding something even better. So she went after it. Her act of disobedience grew out of her doubts about God's goodness.

When the serpent tempted Eve, she was thoroughly deceived (2 Cor. 11:3; 1 Tim. 2:14). Adam, we are told, was not deceived. He knew God was not keeping back a richer experience of life. But when his wife broke God's law, he had no confidence that the goodness of God *as he knew it to that point* would be sufficient to bring a good resolution to the mess Eve had created. He had no experience with God's forgiving nature. To that point, nothing had required forgiveness. But instead of trusting in the depths of God's goodness waiting to be revealed, he solved his problem with his wife by joining her in sin. Eve doubted that God was *good*. Adam doubted that God was *good enough* to overwhelm sin with grace.

To say it another way: our doubting of God began when Eve decided that God might be keeping something good from her, and therefore took steps to enhance her own well-being. When Adam yielded to his wife to keep from losing her, rather than trusting in the goodness of God to handle the dilemma of an already sinful wife, the structure fell firmly into place in the center of the human soul. Each one of us is now a born doubter. And this doubt has been passed on like a virus to every human being since that time, except one.

Finding God means to rest in his goodness through poverty, lost opportunities, and plane crashes. Our calling is to enjoy that confidence and reflect it to others, no matter what happens. But honoring that calling is not easy. We all begin life infected with a lethal disease. Paul called it "the law of sin at work within my members" (Rom. 7:23).

That law, I suggest, is the determined inclination to believe that God is not good, or at least not "good enough," to be fully trusted.

BORN DOUBTERS

From the moment we are born, we are all doubters. The first sound we make is a cry of terror. "What is this world I am entering?" the infant cries. "Will my needs be met? Is anyone here who will always do for me what needs to be done? Can I really be sure that someone will feed me and clothe me and care for me? Can I really rest?"

Nothing in the infant naturally trusts the universe to be fully sensitive to his needs. The child wants *proof*—a full belly, dry clothing, a warm bed, loving attention—and then, only then, will he trust.

Without a natural inclination to assume that the final authority in the world is benevolent, every child from the point of birth knows terror. And as children grow, their experiences of life add to the terror. They may be victims of war or poverty. They may suffer neglect or abuse. But even if they don't experience specific traumas, they are terrorized. Life itself is a trauma, an unpredictable drama that breeds terror.

Doubt of God's goodness creates the terror of aloneness in an unreliable world, which leads to rage against God for doing so little to protect us from suffering.

Initial doubt quickly yields to the terror of facing absolute dependency in an undependable world. Then, just as quickly, the terror slides into rage: "Am I wrong to want what no one provides? I didn't decide to need love that is unavailable. Someone decided it for me, then refused to give it to me. It just isn't fair. My inescapable pain makes me mad!"

At whom? At whomever is responsible for life in the first place. At whomever invites our trust but fails to earn it by immediately responding to all our needs. At whomever represents himself as unconquerably powerful and unstoppably good but doesn't protect us from horrible mistreatment. The infant's rage is directed at his mother and father—and ultimately at God.

To the fallen mind, it makes sense to be mad at God. Without the intervention of God's Spirit, each of us learns to reason like this: "If you're so good, then how come you let that man touch me, or my mother get sick, or my crippled legs have no strength?"

The foundation of the fallen structure is our *doubt* of God's goodness, which creates the *terror* of aloneness in an unreliable world, which leads to *rage* against God for doing so little to protect us from suffering. And then, to make matters worse, when we turn to God for help, he tells us that we're wrong for not already loving him and doing good to others. For many, that's the final straw (Rom. 7:5).

HAVING IT OUT WITH GOD

Neither my terror nor my rage stops me from asking questions; in fact, they drive me to ask more. I know that God will not yield to my impudence and answer them, but still I ask, because something in me *wants* to ask questions, whether I get answers or not. The point of the questions seems to be in the asking. Putting my confusion into words generates a satisfying sense of power that helps me survive the inexplicable madness of life.

Too often my questioning feels less like the curiosity of one eager for instruction, and more like an indignant accusation from one who feels betrayed. As strange and ridiculous as it sounds, I think I want to have it out with God. A perverse energy in my soul *actually wants to challenge God!* The prospect of winning seems dim, but the fight itself feels devilishly invigorating. And even though I expect to be knocked out, I may be able to get in a couple of licks along the way.

Could this energy be the same as the passion that drives Satan? He must know that he is no match for God; he must realize that eventual defeat is certain. But still he wages his battle to usurp God's throne. Why? Is he blinded to his destiny by the fury of his hatred? Does the use of derivative power against the One from whom it is derived generate a heady rush that masquerades as omnipotence; and, like an addictive passion, does the rush keep him going? The most terrible question is this: In my desire to challenge God, do I still bear a likeness to the father of darkness, even though I have been delivered from his family?

MAKING GOD PROVE HIMSELF

Instead of feeling horrified at my own impudence toward God, I sometimes feel smug, wondering how God might choose to defend himself against my well-supported charges that challenge his claim to goodness.

I'm not the first to feel this way. After Job endured more suffering than I'll ever know, he said:

"If only I knew where to find him . . .
I would state my case before him
    and fill my mouth with arguments.
I would find out what he would answer me,
    and consider what he would say." (Job 23:3–5)

In the middle of his suffering, when all happy passions were smothered by grief, something came alive within Job as he courted the idea of challenging God. Nothing more closely masquerades as true vitality than arrogance, and arrogance keeps us from giving ourselves to God in desperate, grateful humility. Perhaps that is why God hates pride above every other sin.

It is the fallen structure within the soul of every man and woman that delights to challenge God, because doing so creates a powerful sense of identity. This evil structure begins with the idea that perhaps God is not good enough to be fully trusted and that we are therefore justified in looking out for ourselves.

WHEN WE DOUBT GOD'S GOODNESS

What happens when we doubt God's goodness, when the trials of life strengthen our doubts to the point where trusting him seems like madness? It is then that self-trust appears entirely reasonable; it seems right but, in fact, leads to death (Prov. 14:12). We become convinced that we must make up for God's deficient involvement in our lives by taking care of a few things on our own.

Sin may be thought of as our effort to supplement what we think are limits to God's goodness. It is trusting our *self* instead of trusting God.

Until we see Christ fully, we will in some measure try to preserve, protect, and develop that fragile thing we call the *self*, that sense of who we are that longs to enjoy love, respect, and meaning. Until our tendency to evaluate God by what we see is exposed and weakened, we will continue looking for *ourselves* with all our heart and soul. The result is that we will never find God.

Sin is simply our effort to supplement what we think are deficiencies in God's goodness. It is trusting our self instead of trusting God.

Instead of trying to solve the problems that plague our lives, we must undermine the fallen structure that supports our problems, a structure built on the arrogant presumption that it is reasonable and right to seek justice for ourselves because God is not good enough to be fully trusted.

Today we see the fruit of this fallen structure as never before. *Self*-preservation, *self*-development, *self*-nourishment, *self*-care, *self*-expression, *self*-protection, *self*-enhancement. These are the final aims of most modern efforts to walk through problems. Move through your problems toward finding *yourself!* Depend on God to help you realize your greatest and most worthy ambition: the enjoyment of your *self!*

The cultural obsession with self is reflected in the recovery movement. In the last few years men and women have been poring over their pasts, determined to recover from their dysfunctional backgrounds, to restore dignity to their violated and badly shamed identities, and to free themselves from codependent relationships by affirming, nourishing, and asserting their intrinsic value. Even the church has bought into the language of recovery. Rather than blushing over our commitment to the god of self, we parade it as an extension of the gospel: "If God loves us, how can we do less than love ourselves? We honor God when we increase our self-esteem."

Are we living in the days Paul warned us about, those last days when "there will be terrible times," times when "people will be lovers of themselves" (2 Tim. 3:1–2) and will be guilty of all the wickedness that flows from self-love? Have we come to that climactic point in history when the essence of evil—love for self above all else—is regarded as the height of virtue?

If so, it is no wonder that God seems more distant from us than ever. The more we understand our own fallen nature, the more we will understand why God won't let us find him.

8
Why God Won't Let Us Find Him

T he fabric of life is woven with tragedy. And in the midst of tragedy, so often God seems absent. Why? Why does God distance himself from us when we need to feel his presence? Why is he silent when we long to hear his voice? Why do we sometimes seek him but not find him?

The answer can be found in our fallen structure. *When we approach God with this structure still in place he will not listen to us.* He refuses to hear a word we say. He distances himself from us. Why? Perhaps if we can see the structure as it really is, then we can begin to understand why God finds it so offensive. At its ugliest, this structure expresses itself in words like these:

"Prove yourself! I doubt your goodness. Look at what has happened in my life and in the lives of people I love. Do you know what it's like living with a constant dread that something terrible might happen? Since you provide me with no guarantee that nothing bad will happen, you need to convince me that you are trustworthy.

"And if you don't, I declare myself free of any obligation to worship or serve you. Why *should* I serve you anyway? Trusting you and obeying your commands does not guarantee what I want to enjoy now.

"For the life of me, I can't see why it's immoral for me to arrange for my own personal comfort, since no one else is. I am a decent person. Stepping on others, violating moral standards, ignoring other people's pain—these are things I don't do. But if I have to do these things to take care of myself, I will.

"And don't you dare tell me I'm wrong for taking care of myself. You haven't proven your goodness to me; therefore, you have no right to rebuke me, much less to claim my trust. If you want to get back on better terms with me, you know what you must do: use your power to make things better. I want to like myself more, hurt less, and feel good about life. All I'm asking you to do is demonstrate the goodness you claim for yourself. Is that so unreasonable? And if you do, I might eventually trust you. I might even say 'thank you' someday."

The sheer danger of talking to God like this is exhilarating. Self-righteous defiance makes us feel big. Our approach to God reflects a proud spirit of concern for ourselves more than a humble spirit that longs to enjoy God. And because we approach God from the foundation of self-righteous, self-serving doubt, God does not listen to us. He will not let us find him.

But it sounds so extreme. Do *Christians* really talk like that? Unbelievers maybe, but Christians? Is that how *I* sometimes approach God? I've been a Christian for more than forty years. Is that energy still inside me? Is it in each of us?

APPROACHING GOD THE WRONG WAY: A PERSONAL ILLUSTRATION

A wrong approach to God can be seen, not only in the big spiritual battles, but also in the everyday decisions of life. Recently, I was faced with a tough choice. The options before me were both attractive, yet I had to choose one and lose the other. Because of the people involved, the loss on either side was significant.

On the morning of the day I had to decide, I woke up thinking about the decision. I prayed for guidance as I showered. I had, of course, been praying for weeks, but I still could not sense any clear direction from God. I felt anxious, cornered by the decision, and eager for guidance.

As the hot water pounded my back, a thought occurred to me: "Maybe I should fast today, at least skip breakfast and lunch, and see if before five o'clock God will make clear which way I should go."

Over the past several years, I have used the discipline of fasting to center my attention on a realm beyond the physical; I have read many stories of respected saints who fasted to hear the voice of God better. The idea seemed appealing. It might be a good way to persuade God to speak up.

But as I resolved to carry out my plans, something felt wrong. I could not suppress a noble whisper within me that said, "That should impress him!"

The fallen structure was at work. My desire for help from God had twisted my thinking to the point where I felt that God *should* help, that his claim to goodness *required* it of him. I was approaching God, but not with an already settled confidence in his goodness. I was not prepared to call him good if he refused to cooperate with my plans. But that is exactly what he calls us to do. He *is* good, whether my brother dies in a plane crash or your son commits suicide.

Now this can be said harshly like a barked command: "Now you listen here. God is good, and you better believe it!" Or it can be said gently, as an invitation to delight in someone whose powerfully loving commitment to us exceeds our wildest dreams.

We may have trouble believing in his goodness—some events in life may introduce us to intense battles with faith that push us to the breaking point—but our struggle to believe that he's good does not change the truth. He is unalterably good. He does not wish me pain. He longs to bless me, and he knows that my happiness depends on my finding him. He has committed both his power and his heart to making me eternally happy. It's the way he goes about honoring his commitment that sometimes unnerves me.

God really can be quite frustrating.
I'm willing to fast, but he likely
won't even notice. What does it take
to get him to cooperate?

As I showered that morning, my soul was not in line with the truth that God is good. I was more interested in a particular *demonstration* of his goodness. I sincerely wanted God's will in this decision, and I was quite willing to go either way. Shouldn't God therefore make clear to me what choice he wanted me to make? Am I wrong to expect my Father to offer guidance?

I confess that I wasn't terribly confident that my fasting would move God to respond. But—and here is the evidence of the fallen structure at work within me—I thought it should! If God failed to respond, then in some hidden region of my soul, I would think that I had a legitimate gripe against God! And rather than feeling broken by the sheer audacity of such a thought, I felt powerful, justified, courageously alone. No emotion creates a more satisfying illusion of noble strength than anger.

As I went back and forth in my mind about the wisdom of fasting, I listened to myself grumble: "God really can be quite frustrating. I'm willing to fast, but he likely won't even notice. What does it take to get him to cooperate?"

The ungodly structure at the root of most of our problems is most clearly evident in our grumbling. When things don't go as we want, we complain that God cannot be trusted with the really important matters in life. And our fellowship with him grows cold.

I was willing to jump through whatever hoops God set up,

but only on the condition that he would respond as I directed. Had I chosen to fast with the prayer that God would clearly direct me, but resolved to praise him for his goodness even if he didn't, then my approach to God, in some way, would have led me to him.

The fallen personality structure within each of us is built on one central lie: *God cannot be trusted with the things that matter most.* We thank him for opening up a parking space in a crowded lot, but we cannot trust him with our souls.

The fallen personality structure within each of us is built on one central lie: God cannot be trusted with the things that matter most.

To the degree that we believe the lie, we take the initiative to secure the blessings we desire, claiming the right to make up for God's indifference by working to preserve whatever we value. When we take the initiative, the results include *pressure to make things happen* ("I've *got* to make my daughter see how wrong she is"), *worry that we might fail* ("I just don't know if I can get through to her"), and *bitterness over the lack of help we receive* ("I can't understand why God isn't doing more to change her into the kind of young woman she ought to be, and no one else is terribly helpful either").

Believing this lie is not new.

EXAMPLES FROM THE BIBLE

In the days of the prophet Isaiah, many Israelites came to Jehovah hoping—as I had done—to bargain with God through fasting. Listen to God's description of their approach: "Day after day they seek me out; they seem eager to know my ways. . . . They ask me for just decisions and seem eager for God to come near them" (Isa. 58:2).

But God told them, "You cannot fast as you do today and expect your voice to be heard on high" when you approach me the way you do (v. 4).

They thought nothing was wrong with their effort to find God. The fault lay with God. God wasn't performing as he should, and they had every right to question his goodness. "Why have we fasted . . . and you have not seen it? Why have we humbled ourselves, and you have not noticed?" (v. 3).

In other words: "God, we've done our part. You are now obligated to demonstrate your goodness by doing what we want done. But you haven't done so. We therefore have a right to lodge a complaint against you!"

Another group of Israelites had the same bad attitude toward God. To them God said, "Although they shout in my ears, I will not listen to them" (Ezek. 8:18). These people could not coerce God to listen to them any more than Esau, with all his tearful pleading, was able to elicit a blessing from his father, Isaac.

God will not listen to me if I approach him proudly, requiring that he prove himself to me.

"I will not listen to them." These are terrifying words. Why won't he listen to them? Will he listen to *me*? Am I shouting in his ears or, as Hosea puts it, am I wailing on my bed, with no hope of finding God (Hos. 7:14)?

From the example of the Israelites, it is clear that God will *not* listen to me if I approach him proudly, requiring that he *prove* himself to me, thinking that I have the *right* to demand him to do things on my behalf. When I value God only because I regard him as useful to my purposes, he will not let me find him.

If we are to find God as he wants to be found, if we are to know him in a way that frees us to live with joy and purpose and self-control, then we must not work primarily to solve our problems. Instead, we must work to dismantle our fallen structure, replacing the foundation of doubt with a rock-solid trust in God.

9
The Foundation of a Solid Structure: Trusting God

D ismantling our fallen structure takes nothing short of a revolution. In a world as immoral as this one, and in people who are as determined as we are to fit into this world, we must hate and destroy the bad before the good can take its place.

Some insist that the new birth gets rid of all the vicious arrogance that defines the old nature, or at least weakens it enough so that it's no longer a bother. They teach that a love for Christ fills our hearts, where it consumes every other affection and anchors us deeply in God's goodness.

Recovery experts teach that shame—the illegitimate message from dysfunctional families that we are bad—is the core "sin" corrupting our efforts to live responsibly and love well. Release from the shame that binds us is taught as the route to maturity and emotional health. Finding God, as these experts have reworked it, means realizing that his love for us frees us to accept ourselves as worthwhile people who can now parade our value as evidence of God's grace.

According to this line of thinking, Christian growth is

nothing more than the development of something good. Nothing left within us needs to be destroyed, nothing morally wicked needs to be exposed and increasingly forsaken. The real internal enemy is not sin, these folks say, but rather a lack of confidence in our own goodness, or a limited awareness of our new identity.

A BLOODY REVOLUTION

But if the fallen structure I am describing in these chapters survives the new birth, if a stubborn inclination to demand that God prove his goodness still lingers within us, then we must anticipate an internal revolution as we seek to find God.

Limited restoration, of course, requires less. If you want to recover from a poor self-image, read self-help books and affirm the good things in yourself. If you are drinking too much, get counseling, join AA, and make yourself accountable to a group. With this limited restoration, you may change your thinking and your behavior, but you will not change what is, at core, wrong with you. Total restoration demands more.

Restoration to rich confidence in God's goodness requires a bloody revolution that introduces a level of pain that doesn't always feel worth it. Dismantling the fallen structure of the human personality—and replacing it with a godly structure— requires that four conditions be met:

• We must be willing to endure internal suffering without knowing when it will end and without the ability to arrange for its relief. We must endure what will seem like the loss of life.

• We must enter that suffering to an unendurable level where every pleasure that earlier brought relief and comfort no longer does so. We must enter that suffering to the level where we become bored with the pleasures that used to relieve the pain. The pleasures of sin must lose their power to relieve our pain.

• We must plead with God's Spirit to answer our cry for mercy by exposing our fallen structure as dangerously evil.

• We must plead with God's Spirit to reveal the sheer beauty of the character of Christ until the opportunity to know him, and to reflect him to others, becomes the stabilizing anchor during life's toughest storms.

COSMETIC CHANGES

Most of us limp along knowing very little of these four conditions. We want relief from pain, we cherish whatever pleasures lift us out of it, we expect the Holy Spirit to affirm our value rather than expose what may be ugly, and we are drawn more to the possibility of personal fulfillment than to the opportunity to know God through suffering.

We must never be satisfied with any movement toward the way things should be that does not also vigorously revolt against the way things are.

Life can move along quite pleasantly without our paying much attention to these four severe-sounding conditions. We can resolve problems, relieve painful feelings, and improve difficult relationships without ever disrupting the fallen structure beneath them. Rooms can be redecorated and even rebuilt on a bad foundation. Cosmetic changes happen all the time in counselors' offices, both Christian and secular, around the world.

Fallen structures remain undisturbed in many of those who pastor, disciple, evangelize, and counsel. I wonder sometimes if their ministry tends to promote more breadth than depth and if the good they do fails to develop the kind of character that can survive the harshest test.

We must never be satisfied with any movement toward the

way things should be that does not also vigorously revolt against the way things are. As we promote God's purposes in this world, we must remain fiercely committed to the destruction of every trace of the enemy within.

FIGHTING THE WRONG ENEMY

The danger of promoting the good without disrupting the bad was illustrated by a college chaplain I know. He told me about some students whose parents had joined 12-step recovery groups to overcome a wide variety of addictions and codependent styles of relating. The parents reported to their children that their troubling behaviors had lost their addictive grip and that they liked themselves better.

But the students did not share their parents' excitement. They found themselves no more eager to visit home than before their parents' recovery. Dad was sober and more pleasant to be with, but his daughter sensed no more of a nourishing connection with him than when he was drunk. Mother was less frantic, better able to say no to unfair demands from others, but her children felt the same absence of tender involvement.

Why? Is it possible that most of us are fighting against the wrong enemy? Do we fight against self-hatred or irresponsibility while a more treacherous enemy goes unchallenged? Would it be better if Dad occasionally drank and Mom continued to give away too much time if, at the same time, they each could find a way to give more of themselves to their children?

That strange blessing might be granted, I submit, if their focus were less on sobriety and self-assertion and more on finding God. Perhaps then they would value *giving* themselves above *finding* themselves, and they would learn to hate whatever interfered with honoring that higher value. Hating what ought to be hated might help them order their lives to reflect God's goodness instead of arranging things to increase their sense of personal well-being. And, as they both found

God, Dad would drink less, and Mom would become more self-disciplined with her time.

People whose priority is to find themselves, either through disciplined obedience or release from shame, recognize no deeper problem within themselves than moral sloppiness or a damaged identity; and therefore, they set out merely to *do better* or to *like themselves more*. They look for healing without ever facing the root disease.

Could it be that using God to solve problems keeps us from facing what is *really* wrong? Are we moving farther away from God's design, feeling excited when we should be broken, hopeful when we should despair? Are we spending our lives repainting rotten walls? Are we, like the leaders in Ezekiel's day, saying "peace" when there is no peace, and covering with whitewash the flimsy walls of our own making (Ezek. 13:10)? If so, this is what the Lord says:

> "In my wrath I will unleash a violent wind, and in my anger hailstones and torrents of rain will fall with destructive fury. I will tear down the wall you have covered with whitewash and will level it to the ground so that its foundation will be laid bare. When it falls, you will be destroyed in it; and you will know that I am the LORD." (Ezek. 13:13–14)

GOD IS GOOD— NO MATTER WHAT HAPPENS

The beginning of a path is always the most important. Miss the entrance, and you never walk the path. Perhaps the narrow gate that opens onto the route toward God, the gate that many Christians think they have walked through but never have, can be found in an idea so simple that we often miss its force:

> *You know you're finding God when you believe that God is good no matter what happens.*

We will know that we have found God when *nothing* can shake our confidence in his unchanging goodness, not:

- Plane crashes that kill loved ones.
- Positive biopsies that shatter dreams.
- Unexpected unemployment that fills every thought of tomorrow with fear.
- Unfaithful spouses that rip your heart to pieces.
- Rebellious children that provoke both unimaginable pain and self-doubt.
- Demanding jobs that keep you moving at a frantic, health-threatening pace.
- Battles with self-hatred that make every mention of identity in Christ sound like mockery.
- Memories of abuse that haunt every waking moment and excite every nightmare.
- Personal failure that shreds the last remnants of hope.
- Difficult decisions in which either direction involves significant loss.
- Consuming loneliness that covers your soul like a fog.

Maintaining our faith in God's goodness in these times is not easy. Like Job, we will cry out in fear and despair. "Where was God during my rape?" cries a victim of one man's evil. "Don't tell me he was there. I already believe that. But why didn't he do anything?" "I didn't know my little boy was playing behind our car. I backed over him and killed him," sobs a young father. "How could a good God allow that?"

No one will conclude that God is good by studying life. The evidence powerfully suggests otherwise. Belief in the goodness of God and the worship that naturally flows from this confidence depends on the revealing work of the Holy Spirit. When he ushers us into the presence of ultimate goodness, when our darkest tragedy is pierced by one glimpse of invisible glory, then faith is born.

And the faith given by God's Spirit makes self-concern lau,,hably unnecessary. We know we're in good hands no matter what comes. And our manner of living reflects our knowledge.

We relax and get on with the purpose of life on this earth—worshiping God and advancing his kingdom.

Every Christian has a relationship with Christ as savior, God as father, and the Holy Spirit as indwelling comforter and guide. With full right, each of us can therefore say, "I have found God" or better, "God has found me."

But in a far richer sense, every Christian must also say, "I am still looking for him." Even Paul longed to know more of Christ, for he was aware that he had not yet apprehended all there was to know about him (Phil. 3:12–14).

The search for God will lead us through struggles, setbacks, and confusion. Confidence in a God who doesn't always make clear what he's doing at any given moment doesn't come easily. It's hard to believe that God fully takes into account our strong desire to be happy. We naturally and unrelentingly think otherwise.

If left to our own way of thinking, every one of us would conclude that God either is bad or doesn't exist.

This natural inclination is what's fundamentally wrong with us. If left to our own way of thinking, every one of us would conclude that God either is bad or doesn't exist, that no God in this universe is good enough to be trusted with the things that matter most. We may ask him to bless our food, but we won't continue to trust him when a loved one betrays us.

As we look at how God treats some of his children, even those who abandon themselves fully to his care, we're not impressed. And when God looks bad, sin looks good. The determination to take matters into our own hands seems entirely moral.

This doubt has been passed on like a virus to every human being—except One. And that Person, having lived a life of absolute confidence in the Father, gave us reason to replace our doubt with faith. Jesus Christ has made his Father known and delights in continuing to do so. We find God through Christ. There is no other way.

Now if it is true that all our problems are rooted in the suspicion that God isn't good (or isn't good enough), then the only way through our problems is to know Christ better and thereby to find God. Remember the principle:

You know you're finding God when you believe that God is good no matter what happens.

Or, in other words:

Finding God is developing, through Christ, an unshakable confidence in God's absolute goodness and perfect love no matter what we may experience in this life.

Finding God means to rest in his goodness through poverty, blindness, and plane crashes. Finding God means to face all of life, both good and bad, with a spirit of trust. We have a higher calling than finding joy in good things and working through bad things: we must reflect confidence in God in *all* our relationships and activities, in *all* our joys and sorrows.

WHEN GOD REVEALS HIMSELF TO US

When we approach God with the attitude of an unworthy beggar whose only hope is another's kindness—like the prodigal son, who knew his own sin, yet trusted in his father's love to forgive him—then God tears away the veil that separates us and runs to meet us with a ring, a robe, and a full banquet, stunning us with his eager longing to enjoy a close relationship with us. With his generous heart overflowing, he refuses to withhold anything from us that will help us know him better. In his own sovereign way, without consulting with us, he patiently arranges things in our lives so that we experience him as the satisfier of our souls, as our loving bridegroom, as a good God who never intends anything but our joy.

In Malachi's day, there was a group of Israelites who came to God humbly, begging his forgiveness. And God took notice. Rather than shutting his ears, he "listened and heard" (Mal. 3:16). He paid attention to them as they honored him in their conversation. Those two words, *listened* and *heard*, reveal a God who stops when he hears his name called, who turns to see who called him, then bends down, putting his ear close to the speaker's mouth so as not to miss a word.

God wants to be found. He delights to be known. He rejoices when we are close to him. But our search for him must be on *his* terms. And those terms involve a radical shift away from our natural inclination to evaluate his goodness. He will not tolerate anyone sitting in judgment of him. We are not the judges. We are rather the judged, the forgiven, and the invited. "Come, taste and see that the Lord is good."

I long to taste more of the Lord's goodness. But I will not get it as long as I think he is obligated to resolve my problems. God will not let me find him if I regard him as nothing more than a useful tool for obtaining my own desires.

Therefore, I must cooperate with God in dismantling the fallen structure on which so much of my life is built. The shaky foundation of doubt must be replaced with the firm foundation of trust.

A GODLY FOUNDATION

Think for a moment what it would be like to turn toward God with a different foundation. Imagine relating to God with complete contentment, joyfulness, and eagerness to give. Get some idea of the difference in building your life on a godly foundation—the foundation of "I Believe God"—rather than the fallen one—"I Doubt God." For the moment, don't worry about how to put it in place; just realize how passionately you long for it to be there:

- You no longer *doubt*, but *believe in* his goodness.
- You no longer feel *terror*, but feel *calm* at his words: "I'll

never leave you. You can walk through the valley of the shadow of death with me. Be of good cheer. You'll have trouble in this world but I've overcome it. Your story has an ending too happy to describe. Trust me."

• You no longer feel *rage*, but want to *worship*. "God, you alone are worthy. I believe that those who love you will never be ashamed."

Imagine what it would be like to say the following words from Habakkuk and mean them! (I've added a few phrases in italic to bring this passage home.)

Though the fig tree does not bud
    and I am alone;
  and there are no grapes on the vines,
    and I can find no joy in my world right now;
though the olive crop fails
    and I have nothing to soothe my open wounds;
  and the fields produce no food,
    and I'm out of a job or hate the one I have;
though there are no sheep in the pen
    and no one warms me on cold nights
  and no cattle in the stalls
    and I have no tangible basis for feeling secure,
yet I will rejoice in the LORD,
  I will be joyful in God my Savior.
The Sovereign LORD is my strength;
  he makes my feet like the feet of a deer,
  he enables me to go on the heights.

(Hab. 3:17–19)

Shifting our foundation from doubt to confidence, from terror to enjoyment, from rage to worship will occur only when something stirs within us that makes us long, more than anything else, to build our lives on the reality of God.

But we're not there yet. No one is, not fully.

With doubt, terror, and rage filling our hearts, we turn to

others, not to love them, but to get from them at least a little of what we need. Bent on relief from our pain and revenge against God, we enter into relationships with the desperate cry that seems so reasonable: "I need you!" And that cry moves us into the first floor of the fallen structure.

10
First Floor: I Need You

When our doubts about God create a terror of living ("What will happen tomorrow? Will I be all right?") and a rage at God ("Why won't he come through for me as I want him to?"), we then turn to others, not to love them, but to demand that they give us something to make our lives pleasant, or at least more bearable. Something has to be done, but we can't count on God.

We may hide our demands of others behind a veil of civility and kindness, but our real agendas sound like this:

- Give me a break.
- Don't put me in a position where I have to be stronger than I am right now. Don't require me to grow.
- Don't make me feel bad when I fail. Convince me that you still accept me even when I hurt you.
- Respect me whether I deserve it or not.
- Be sensitive to my need for affirmation and to how I'd like to receive it.
- Support me in my stumbling efforts to be responsible, and understand how my pain makes responsible living difficult.

What we should gratefully receive as mercies, we demand as rights. We have been encouraged to pay such close attention to our hurts and longings that little else seems quite as important. Rather than asking ourselves what we still are able to give *despite* our pain, we focus on our pain, using the latest jargon to describe it ("My dysfunctional behavior is shame-based and codependent") and trying to work through it according to current experts' latest insights. In the name of openness and vulnerability, we parade our aches and pains with the self-congratulating air of a noble struggler, giving little thought to the impact we make for good or bad on others. *We* are the point. *Our* welfare comes first. "After all I've been through," we say, "it's my turn to be cared for. *I need you!*"

PUTTING OURSELVES FIRST

None of us is immune to putting ourselves first. I don't think I've learned anything about myself that has more surprised and appalled me than how reflexively I put my own needs first.

Within days of my brother's death, I spoke at his memorial service. As I prepared my few comments on behalf of our family, I prayed that God would use my stumbling tongue in this difficult situation to encourage others to trust in the goodness of God no matter what might happen in their lives. I wanted to give.

At one point during my talk, I noticed that a phrase I had just used was especially rich. As any experienced public speaker might do, I paused to let that phrase sink in. During that three-second pause, I heard these words run through my mind, "I'm doing a pretty good job. That was a good pause." Immediately, I felt slapped in the face by the realization that at that moment I cared more about how I was performing than about how meaningfully I was ministering.

That night I wept bitterly. I grieved that even at my brother's funeral I couldn't escape the wretched power of pride.

I had come to an audience filled with friends wanting to share our grief, and I wanted them to applaud my speaking ability. Without words, I had said to them, "I need you. Please stroke my ego and help me to feel good about the talents God has given me."

I want what I want when I want it.
Is there a higher value?

God's grace frees me *from* needing to be better than I am and frees me *to* face what I'm really like without giving up. The shock of seeing the truth about myself enables me to embrace God's grace more fully.

THE CAUSE OF CODEPENDENCY

So often I feel that someone is obligated to give me the food my hungry heart craves and the water that will relieve my parched soul. If someone fails to respond, I feel justified in taking measures to fill my emptiness. The morality of those measures is determined by their effectiveness. If I get what I want, then my measures are moral. I want what I want when I want it. Is there a higher value?

Because God only responds to prayer that furthers his purposes, I can't manipulate him. So I turn away from God toward you, and with practiced skill evoke from you what I want. Thus I fall into what is called codependency: manipulating someone else to behave in ways that make me feel safe and secure. The pattern is not only neurotic; it is wicked. The cure for codependency goes far beyond assessing my needs and admitting that I can't meet them; it also requires me to repent of trusting God so poorly that I demand from you what only he can give.

Whether I consciously feel my pain or not, I am far more aware of my feelings than of yours. Until I have complete confidence that God knows my emptiness and sorrow and is able to take care of me, I will continue to look after my interests before I bother with yours. Of course, I'll never get around to worrying about you, because my worries will never quit. Can't you see? I *need* you, more than you need me. If you could climb inside my soul and feel the anguish there, then you would understand.

ONE OF TWO PATHS

When we sort through the way we relate to one another, we will find that we are walking one of two paths: *Either* we are more interested in what others can do for us *or* we are more concerned with what we have to give to them. A good relationship happens when both parties consistently walk the second path.

It is not enough to decide that the second path is better and then try hard to walk it. Until the foundation of our fallen structure crumbles, we cannot make ourselves nicer people by a mere act of will. To attempt it creates frustration, and occasionally, in folks who think their efforts successful, it breeds smugness.

Either we are more interested in what others can do for us, or we are more concerned with what we have to give to them.

Many people agree that trying harder to be nice will not work, but then they choose a disastrous alternative. They think that learning to love themselves first makes it possible to love someone else later. One practical problem with this plan is our bottomless need to feel loved. Once we start working to love ourselves, we never get around to loving others. We may learn to be more assertive with them, but we don't really love them.

We must neither rely on mere effort to love better nor

make it top priority to arrange for the love we need. Rather, we must face up to how bad we hurt, how deeply we long for someone to relieve that hurt, and how poorly we trust God to look after our interests.

Next, we must give up any hope of finding a method that will allow us to trust God better. We must simply do our best to obey, to pray, and to soak in his Word and then, when months, perhaps years, pass by without any visible change in our experience of him or our dealings with others, we will be introduced to deeper capacities within us for passionate trust. We will more keenly feel our intense contempt for God, we will recognize our awful demand that someone take care of us, and we will become aware of a deep longing to trust God. Only then will we see clearly how natural it is to require something from others rather than to give something to them.

When we live to get from others (and everyone does who suspects that God isn't good), the results are always the same: inevitable disappointment, temporary fulfillment, and bitter loneliness. When we doubt God and turn away from him to cry to others, "I need you," we never stop crying.

THE GODLY STRUCTURE: I LOVE YOU

But think how it could be different. Our Lord once said to his disciples, "A new command I give you: Love one another" (John 13:34). This command had been given centuries earlier (see Lev. 19:18). What made it new when our Lord gave it?

Right after he said those words, he followed it with, "As I have loved you, so you must love one another." Apparently something about the way he loved them, which had not been visible till he literally walked with them, was supposed to give new depth to their love for each other.

When Jesus Christ came to earth, he exhibited his own resources as well as the Father's. We now could see with clearer vision what God is really like. Until then, the command to love was just that—a command.

But now, with a fuller revelation of the goodness of God revealed in the grace that came by Christ, we see the command as an invitation to a party, a party where we are the guests and Christ is the host. He provides the food, and every bit of conversation reflects our sheer fascination with him. If I obey his command and love you, he discloses himself to me (John 14:21, 23). He pulls back the curtain and gives me a glimpse of the party I will soon enjoy. After a few glimpses of that party, I want to see my fallen structure dismantled. I might even be willing to bury the hatchet with some long-time enemies.

I am now beckoned to replace *doubt* and its companions, terror and rage, with a *confidence* in God's character that frees me to relax and trust (see Isa. 30:15). I can then do a little better job of moving toward others without demanding what God has already given. Because I am protected better than the president, I can move about freely, almost recklessly, in this otherwise terrifying world. Instead of saying "I need you," I say, "I want to give something good to you. I want you to relax in the strength that is slowly freeing me to remain confident and hopeful no matter how bad I feel or what struggles come my way."

Confidence in God and hope in his provision do not, in this life, always reflect themselves in a breezy joy. Confident, hopeful people are marked by perseverance and a refusal to seek illegitimate relief in the midst of their ongoing struggles.

ABLE TO GIVE

A young single woman whose walk with the Lord is both disciplined and rich wrote these words to me after having been in counseling for many months: "I often wonder if any change at all took place last year. I'm so aware of how I protect myself as I relate to others, and I want it to be different. I easily get down on myself, and God's grace seems distant. And yet I'm aware that there is a deep conviction within me that yes, I can give. This is not heaven, and that's why I need him so desperately, in order to live in the pain and yet still love and give."

The only evidence of change she can see as she looks at her life is her deepened desire to give. I find myself wanting to shake her happily and shout, "Don't you see? That a woman once committed only to herself now wants to give is a miracle! It's the kind of change God is after—and it's happening in your life. Let your heart sing. God is at work!"

But it's hard to sing when battles with loneliness and discouragement and self-contempt continue. It's tempting to postpone the celebration till these problems clear up, till we're enjoying meaningful relationships and feeling encouraged by affirmation.

In her letter, she told how she had decided to help clean her four-year-old nephew's room and then to play ball with him, a decision made at a point of nearly total despair over feeling alone and unwanted. Her sister, she reported, was tired and needed some help.

Reflecting later, she wrote: "It seems like such a small thing as I write this. And yet, there have been numerous scenes like this one since then, where I've experienced *a shift in the direction of my heart* [emphasis mine] and then been able to move toward someone else with a desire to give."

This young woman has moved from "I need you" to "I give to you." It's a move we all need to make. But if we refuse to make that move, we will find ourselves moving inevitably from "I need you" to "I hate you."

11
Second Floor: I Hate You

T he second floor of the fallen structure is obvious. If we ask someone for bread, and think it should be given to us, we'll be offended if it's not. Blocked goals, especially when we think them necessary for our survival, generate anger.

COMPETING DESIRES

Brian, a thirty-eight-year-old chemist, led an organized life. Discipline was his highest virtue. The structure he built around his life kept out the pain of a father who had never connected with him. "If I just do things right, I'll make it" was his motto. Relating deeply to anyone never crossed his mind. He assumed that others should cooperate with his worthy goal of doing things right.

One evening, he told his wife, Lois, that he needed to return to work after dinner. In her mind, that meant 6:30 or 7:00 p.m. In his, "after dinner" meant 6:30 p.m. She ran an errand with the car and returned a few minutes before 7:00. Brian met her at the door with an angry glare, ripped the keys out of her hand, and stormed out to the car. Lois had no idea what she had done wrong. She didn't realize the function Brian's structured life served.

Brian lived a structured life in order to protect himself from the pain of uninvolvement. In his thinking, if he did everything he should, no one would be able to criticize him, and he'd never have to admit how badly he longed for the relationship he'd never had. That night, Lois had unwittingly blocked his goal. In his mind, she was stripping away his one chance to live without pain. And for doing so, he hated her.

This is exactly what James meant when he wrote: "What causes fights and quarrels among you? Don't they come from your desires that battle within you? You want something but don't get it" (James 4:1–2).

To say we're merely offended is an understatement. When someone can give us what we need but refuses, we are more than offended—we're outraged! The veneer of civility may prevent us from expressing our rage violently or vulgarly, but it does not remove the intensity of our fury. Counselors who go after buried resentment reliably have their digging rewarded. It's there in all of us. We are an angry lot.

THE ROOTS OF ANGER

But it is a serious mistake to deal with our anger without getting down to its roots. We prefer to think that we can overcome anger through controlling it or learning to identify and accept the hurt beneath it. Few counseling sessions go by without the counselor saying something like, "I wonder if your anger reflects a longing for more intimacy than your spouse [friend, parent] is providing. Perhaps you need to realize that your anger is really hiding hurt and loneliness. I want you to consider sharing how hurt you feel with the one at whom you're so angry."

Anger, the deep, smoldering kind that boils to the surface with cutting remarks and coldly distancing behaviors, has its roots in our attitude toward God. Anger always reflects a worse problem than the immediate cause. If, rather than doubting him, we trusted God to look after all our legitimate interests and needs, and if we regarded God's willingness to do so as a reflection of his kindness more than our value, then mistreatment from another, no matter how severe, would only generate righteous anger, never the scheming, vicious, murderous anger that delights to destroy.

When our doubts about God prompt us to cry angrily to others for help, the hatred we feel toward those who let us down is always the wrong kind. And worse, it is tenacious. We can't get rid of it until we change our minds about God. We may suppress it or hide it behind forcibly chosen acts of kindness, but still it remains within us, at full strength, in all its ugly passion.

When someone can give us what we
need but refuses, we are more than
offended—we're outraged!

The sinful nature, which believes God is not worthy of trust and therefore demands help from others, always bears fruit that destroys relationship. Look at Paul's list in Galatians 5:19–21. He writes: "the acts of the sinful nature are obvious: . . . hatred, discord, jealousy, fits of rage, selfish ambition, dissensions, factions, and envy."

Building life on a fallen personality structure creates enormous problems with anger. Beneath most symptoms of psychological disorder, such as eating disorders, sexual perversion, and depression, lies a reservoir of seething fury fed by springs of demanding from others, which in turn are fed by the even deeper and more vile spring of doubting (and therefore hating) God.

THE GODLY STRUCTURE: I ACCEPT YOU

Imagine what it might be like to develop a confidence in God that frees us to come to others demanding nothing from them, and feeling far more passionate about the opportunity to give others a taste of God than to receive something we want.

Think of the power that would be released if someone who had let you down saw in your eyes a tender passion that burned more brightly than anger or hurt. The power to love rather than hate reflects the energy of Christ, a holy passion that reveals the Father's goodness as irresistibly appealing. Shifting from "I hate you" to "I care about you" could mend broken families and bring joy where once there was only sorrow.

Carrie struggled with severe depression. During one counseling session, her husband, Brent, reassuringly laid his hand on her knee. She stiffened. I explored her reaction.

Brent, it seems, had the habit of tenderly patting her whenever she expressed disappointment in anything. He never explored her pain, never talked with her about the best way to handle it, never listened to the full story behind her hurt. He was terrified to face anything in his wife he couldn't handle. She was furious. But she hid it behind a bland smile.

I challenged the smile. She eventually acknowledged her rage, then faced her desperate need that Brent understand, accept, and protect her the way no one—not her father, not God—had ever done. When she saw that her greatest disappointment was directed toward God, she felt broken. She came to him in deep repentance, spent meaningful time in Scripture, and admitted to Brent how terrified and hateful she had felt toward him and toward God.

Because of God's work in Carrie's heart, she was freed to give *to* Brent instead of trying to get *from* him. And the change in Carrie helped Brent move more meaningfully toward her.

Making that shift in thinking requires that the more basic elements in the structure be disrupted and shattered. With these three elements in place—I doubt God, I need you, I hate you—our relationships cannot work. Conflict, tension, and distance are inevitable. And when things break down, rather than admitting our failure and tracing it back to our refusal to trust God, our next move is *away* from depending on others *to* tinkering with our insides. We begin to rearrange the way we look at ourselves in the hope that we can make life a satisfying experience without ever having to trust God. And thus we arrive at the third floor of our fallen structure.

12
Third Floor: I Hate Me

N o one comes to God on his or her own. We rather do exactly the opposite. Even Christians who have already been drawn to Christ and now have hearts that seek after him find ways to avoid absolute trust. We insist that there *must* be a way to make life work using material and strategies we have at hand. We are determined to do all that we can to make coming to God unnecessary.

Trusting God as fully as he commands is as unnatural as an infant, already bonded to his mother, trusting a stranger. In both instances, an agressive, hostile shyness must be overcome. When something presses us to reverse that shyness, we resist. A baby greets the outstretched arms of a friendly neighbor by screaming or clinging to her mother's shoulder. We push away God's outstretched arms and work to continue believing that we can make it on our own. We deny our longings; we indulge in available pleasures; we develop natural talents to win approval, money, or fame; and we use anger to feel powerful. The list is limited only by our depraved ingenuity.

All our strategies, however, have at least one thing in

common: *They all are efforts to avoid the despair that sets in when we realize that no earthly relationship will give us what we need.* Disappointing relationships should have the power to drive us to fall face down, before God, begging mercy and comfort. But that rarely happens, and never without the Spirit's work.

HATING OURSELVES

When a relationship sours, when someone on whom we are depending cannot do for us what needs to be done, we first hate them, and then we hate ourselves.

We insist that there must be a way to make life work using material and strategies we have at hand.

Laura struggles with low self-esteem. Her recovery group affirms her value and encourages her to be more assertive in her relationships. They repeatedly remind her of her identity in Christ. But still a vague disgust for herself lingers.

Laura's parents, the people on whom she naturally depended for love and support, badly failed her. Laura's mother resented her husband, and her bitterness spilled over onto the children. Laura's dad was either distant or mean, except for the times he fondled her. Laura hated her parents. But hating them did not relieve her misery.

Every child works hard to make sense of her world. Why am I treated so badly? What can I do to make things better? If a child admits the obvious truth that her mistreatment by those who should love her is *their* fault, not hers, she loses hope. "If Mom and Dad don't love me, who will? I'm lost."

Like so many, Laura escaped the terror of hopelessness by blaming herself for her parents' failures. She began to think that her failings caused her parents' abusive treatment. "No wonder they hated me," she thought. "I was so uncooperative.

Something is very wrong with me; otherwise, Mom and Dad wouldn't be so mean. If I can figure out what is wrong and correct it, then they'll love me."

Now Laura had a plan to make her life better: she determined to find out what was wrong with her and work on it. She believed that her own flaws caused others to reject her; and if they were corrected, she assumed, then others would love her. And that belief gave her hope that she could one day make life work without ever turning to God. Her self-hatred protected her from facing the fact that no one would ever completely satisfy the hunger of her heart.

But Laura's plan (to make herself lovable and hide whatever might be rejected) *required* her to believe that her flaws fully explained why others didn't love her as she wanted. A poor self-image became *useful* to Laura in surviving a disappointing world where she didn't trust God. The affirmation of her support group never dealt with the depraved function of her low self-esteem.

NOBODY CARES

Hating someone who lets us down is an easily understood reaction. They *should* have treated us better. What's the matter with them, anyway?

At some point, though, it dawns on us that *no one* provides what we need. No one is fully sensitive to our hurts and fears. No one cares for us with a love that allows us to relax fully. Then we realize that perhaps nobody ever will. And a lurking despair—what the Germans call "angst"—escapes the dungeon of our soul's darkest corner and envelops us with its cold realism: "You are alone," it whispers, "and there is no hope of community, love, or meaning."

That moment when the soul first shudders in the presence of despair is an opportunity to find hope in God. But none of us moves in that direction under our own power. We are remarkably determined to put our lives together with our own resources. The urge to trust in ourselves is addictive—and it is the root of all other addictions.

At some point it dawns on us that no one provides what we need.

With devilish wisdom, we find a way that just might lead us out of darkness into the marvelous light of living happily with unbowed heads. We recapture hope by thinking along these lines: "Perhaps the reason no one is relating to me as I want can't be entirely explained by their deficiencies. Perhaps something about me keeps people from wanting to meet my needs. Perhaps if I can fix myself, people will like me and life will be good." And with renewed hope, we set out to find something about ourselves that explains why we are so often disappointed and mistreated:

- I'm not feminine enough.
- I'm too gullible.
- It's wrong to be angry like I've been.
- I must be kinder.
- I'm too reflective. When I think deeply, people laugh at me. I'll just be friendly in a shallow sort of way.
- My longing for affection made me vulnerable to abuse. I shouldn't want affection so badly.
- I'm not very cooperative. I'll try to do what everyone wants me to do.

WORKS SALVATION

Can you see how clever Satan is? Something about us *does* block relationship with God and with everybody else. We *are* unattractive! Satan brings us close to that truth and then deftly steers us in a hopelessly wrong direction. Selfishness, which does make us unattractive, never gets the blame. Or if it does, we think of it as something that needs to be corrected rather than forgiven.

All of this is nothing more than a hell-inspired setup to depend on a "works salvation": Here's something to do, and if you do it well enough, you'll find life. We, therefore, learn to hate ourselves, and then try desperately to overcome a bad self-image. A bad self-image serves a useful function for proud people. It is more than a reflection of shameful treatment by others. A bad self-image absorbs the shock of disappointment in our relationships and converts it into an energy to improve ourselves. It places the blame for our mistreatment on something within us that we can correct; it restores hope by suggesting that we will be treated better if we work hard to improve ourselves.

We prefer to see ourselves as wounded
in our relationships, not sinful before
a holy God.

Many Christians have rightly recognized how a bad self-image generates the terrible pressure to perform. But they wrongly assume that its root is self-hatred. They teach that if we can overcome our hatred for ourselves and learn to rest in God's unconditional love, the pressure to measure up will vanish and we will lead happy, productive, meaningful lives.

This reasoning has a serious flaw: the root problem behind the pressure to perform is not self-hatred, but rather the determination to handle disappointment without ever turning to God, without ever acknowledging personal evil, and without ever gratefully accepting mercy. We prefer to see ourselves as wounded in our relationships, not sinful before a holy God.

A MASTER CHESS PLAYER

Satan is a master chess player who outmaneuvers everyone but God. He sees to it that we explain the abuse we suffer from others by finding a deficiency within ourselves. Having developed a usefully bad self-image, we set to work on correcting it.

Christian counselors rightly object that too many people are operating under intense pressure to perform. They declare that the gospel relieves us of the need to measure up to anyone's standards to win relationship. This statement is correct, but again Satan blocks it with a countermove. He intensifies the feelings of self-hatred always associated with the pressure to perform, but then he directs attention away from their place in the fallen structure. Rather than letting us see those feelings as a natural product of doubting God, then needing and inevitably hating others, he encourages us to focus on self-hatred as the root problem. We then define ourselves as victims of dysfunctional backgrounds who have been afflicted with bad self-images.

Counseling too often identifies those bad feelings, encourages us to get in touch with them and to understand how they came to be, and then highlights the love of Jesus as the best way to overcome them. The cross is thereby stripped of its atoning merit and instead is granted the ongoing value of providing affirmation for people who need to accept themselves. The suffering Savior is reduced to an inspiring symbol that helps us realize our worth. After all, would Jesus go through all that pain for worthless people? Developing self-love becomes the issue. We look to God, not to find him, but to use him. God recedes to the shadows, like a faithful butler. And sin becomes, at best, a secondary issue. Satan, the master chess player, has us cornered. Checkmate!

THE GODLY STRUCTURE: I JUDGE ME

But think what it would be like to judge ourselves honestly, to admit our failure to love and to trust God as he deserves to be trusted, and to be confident of God's forgiveness and transforming power.

Suppose we looked at our self-hatred not merely as a

painful burden to be overcome but as a devious strategy to keep alive our hope that life would work if we could only do better. And then, once we recognized the unnecessary pressure created by that strategy, suppose we saw ourselves not merely as self-hating victims who need affirmation, but as God-doubters who wrongly demand that others come through for us. If we saw our wicked, stubborn violation of God's design, then we would value the cross as the place where God, through his Son, took on our sins and forgave us. And we would see that he continues to forgive us every day of our lives until the day when there will be nothing left to forgive.

Either we live under pressure to grow, or we celebrate grace.

Picture yourself looking back on a difficult childhood, including perhaps horrible abuse, and freely admitting how painful it was and how much you hated those who mistreated you. What would it be like if you were able to give up your energetic commitment to preserve yourself? What would it be like if you desperately desired to be whole, beautiful, and good, but fully trusted God to give you all the desires of your heart? Can you see that you would no longer blame yourself for what happened? You would not develop a poor self-image. Rather, you would enter your pain with the courage of trust and hope in God. Knowing that you are fully forgiven, you would admit your failure to love. You would move from "I hate me" to "I judge me" and then continue on in the strength of forgiveness and hope. "In repentance and rest is your salvation; in quietness and trust is your strength" (Isa. 30:15).

The mature Christian judges himself, not with the spirit of self-hatred, but with the eager desire to conform more fully to the image of Christ. Assessing oneself for the purpose of growing has nothing to do with a contemptuous and obsessive search for evil motives, nor is it prompted by an urge to defend oneself or to prove oneself worthy.

After speaking at my brother's memorial service, I was overcome with remorse over my self-centered pride in my effective "speaker's pause." With that awareness of failure, I could have moved either toward self-hatred leading to angry pressure or toward self-judgment leading to confession and dependence. Had I beaten myself with condemnation that could be relieved by vowing never again to be that selfish, the pressure to improve would have developed. Instead, I admitted the ugliness within me and cried, "Oh, wretched man that I am!" And I remember saying to myself, "I might as well give up on my sanctification." When I later voiced that lament to my father, he commented, "It's about time." He was suggesting that I give up the proud pressure to improve my character.

When we become aware of our failure, we can move toward either self-hatred or self-judgment. When we do no more than condemn ourselves, we fall into the trap of self-hatred and feel terrible pressure to do better.

Either we live under pressure to grow, or we celebrate grace. When I became aware of my self-centeredness at Bill's memorial service, the enjoyment of Christ's acceptance gave rise within me to a deeper longing to be like Christ, a longing that intensified dependence on God's Spirit and, at the same time, weakened my internal demand to be better. I no longer *needed* to be better; I *wanted* to be.

It comes more naturally to hate ourselves and be driven by pressure to improve, than to judge ourselves in a way that leads to a celebration of grace. And with that terrible pressure pushing us, we look for a way to survive, to feel alive in a world that has no life to give.

13
Fourth Floor: I Will Survive

Nothing is wrong with wanting to solve our problems, just as nothing is wrong with wanting to enjoy sexual pleasure or a good meal. The difficulty comes when a legitimate desire becomes a final goal, when eliminating internal struggles or changing painful circumstances or feeling good about ourselves becomes our top priority. When desires become final goals, we chase after them with a fanatic zeal that not only blurs moral boundaries but also drains us of energy for pursuing anything else. We forget our higher calling.

OUR HIGHER CALLING

I once counseled a woman struggling with obsessive thoughts. Very few waking moments passed without a flood of bizarre thoughts racing uncontrollably through her mind, many of them sexual, some plainly evil. Understandably, she wanted to relax mentally, to think normally. She wanted her problem with obsessive thoughts solved.

Since the thoughts began, nearly three years earlier, she had pursued every available avenue in search of relief. One therapist had cast out demons; a psychiatrist had prescribed medications; a counselor had looked at how her motivation had been shaped by earlier trauma; still another counselor had tried mind-control techniques.

If I suffered from her problem, I too would try every form of help I could find in the same spirit that I would run to my dentist with a throbbing molar. Please don't misunderstand what I've said: *It is not wrong to work actively to overcome problems.* It is not wrong to take medicine that might relieve obsessive symptoms or depression, no more than it is wrong to ask your dentist to repair a broken tooth.

It *is* wrong, however, to focus so much effort on solving our problems that we lose sight of our higher calling to find God in the midst of our problems. It *is* wrong to seek solutions to our problems with all our heart, soul, mind, and strength and to forget that continued trials provide a unique opportunity for us to develop confidence in God's goodness. It *is* wrong to depend on remedies that remove an opportunity to know God better.

I struggle with insomnia. Occasionally, I take a pill to help me sleep. I would not refuse help from a sleep disorder specialist. I see nothing un-Christian about profiting from a specialist's expertise—and getting a good night's sleep.

But I hesitate. Some of my richest and most productive times with the Lord occur at 2:00 A.M. after tossing in bed for three frustrating hours. I'm not certain what to do about my sleeplessness, but I am certain that a commitment to find Christ must be stronger than my desire for sleep.

MASTER OF MY FATE

A determined commitment to overcome life's difficulties is wrong on another count: it usually reflects a confidence in our own ability to solve our problems. We think we have the wherewithal to take care of ourselves. Maybe that's why God must first humble us to encourage us to move toward him.

With jaw firmly set and tightly clenched fists waving at

God, we stand tall and declare with poet William Ernest Henley, "I am the master of my fate; I am the captain of my soul." And with the energy of that sentiment coursing through our blood, we move into life, determined to survive.

This familiar sentiment is found not only in the blood of wealthy atheists or successful athletes. Although we may not put it in the dramatic words of the proud poet, *our* attitude is stained with a similar arrogance. We scramble to figure out an effective plan of action when difficulty strikes.

When we pursue the satisfaction God
provides more than we pursue God,
we get neither.

I have often been a guest on radio call-in shows. The calls that come follow a reliable two-part pattern: first, the caller describes a troubling situation ("My husband won't take spiritual leadership in our home" or "I'm out of work"), then she asks, "What should I do?" She assumes that there is always something one can do to improve the situation. If I were to say something like, "No matter what you do, it will have no real value until you are more committed to knowing the Lord than straightening out whatever is wrong in your life," many people would indignantly tell me that they *do* love the Lord—that that's not the problem. They just need to know what is best to do in their particular situation.

If I were to press a bit further and ask what they would like to see happen, they would answer, I suspect, that they want something bad to change to something good: a husband to become a committed Christian, a good job to become available. Or, if circumstances failed to improve, they would want to experience peace and joy in spite of continued problems. I'm no different. We don't want to know God better; knowing him really isn't the point of our questions. Rather, we want to use him to get what we want.

Knowing God, of course, does generate many blessings now, including unpredictable seasons of peace and joy. And one day those who know him will enjoy unimaginably upscale living in a city without crime and a garden without weeds. Then the peace will be complete and the joy constant. Now, we must enjoy the blessings when they come and persevere when they are absent. We must have the courage to continue when all good feeling is gone; we must call him good and remain faithful when we have absolutely no sense of his presence. To do so will sometimes feel like walking through wet cement. But still we must pursue him.

When we pursue the satisfaction God provides more than we pursue God, we get neither. The richest pleasures are reserved for those who long for intimacy with the one they love and move toward that person for the sheer joy that deepened familiarity brings. Knowing the cook can be an even greater pleasure than enjoying his food. Heaven includes both.

But that thinking is hard to grasp. Encouragement to know God better sounds irrelevantly religious, particularly when one blessing would change our lives into a far more pleasant experience. Think how happy we would be if God would give us:

- a negative biopsy
- a good night's sleep
- a sober husband
- one day of feeling good
- less anxiety
- a quiet mind
- an improved relationship with an estranged child
- a loved one's salvation
- hope rather than suicidal feelings
- reduced attraction to a hated perversion

Advice to trust God can sound so anemic. How would you react to a counselor who said: "Be still before him. Do whatever is right: don't nag your husband, don't drink to relieve financial worries, don't scramble for solutions. Do what is right in a spirit of quietness and rest."

Hurting people want practical help; they want clear suggestions on what to do that could either change their circumstances or help them feel better. But notice this: the assumption that something can always be done to make things better reflects an even deeper, more subtle assumption that *we can do it*: we can make our lives more satisfying, more fulfilling.

But we can't. Depending on our talent, wealth, and opportunity, we may make life more comfortable and temporarily pleasurable. But rich fare that nourishes the soul comes only from God. As Christians, we have the resources to obey God, but not to provide ourselves with life. Only God can do that. Therefore we must devote ourselves to obedience and then trust God for satisfaction. It's a rather old-fashioned concept, but one worth keeping, because some problems, like Paul's thorn in the flesh, will not disappear. They weren't meant to.

CALLING THE ARROGANT BLESSED

The presumption that we have resources to solve our problems has a long and dishonorable history. At the very end of Old Testament history, when the evidence that the Jews could not build a prospering nation was strong enough to warrant humility, they boasted, "It is futile to serve God. What did we gain by carrying out his requirements and going about like mourners before the LORD Almighty?" (Mal. 3:14). (There's the foundation of the fallen structure: doubts about God's goodness plus rage directed against him.)

Listen to their next sentence: "But now we call the arrogant blessed" (3:15). Catch the meaning of these remarkable and thoroughly stupid words. The Jews were saying something like this: "There really is no point in doing things God's way. Nothing we do seems to make him feel obligated to make life go as we want. So, even though we may be angry and uncertain of how to get along with ourselves and others, we're still better off trusting our own resources as we try to make it in this crazy world. Our happiness depends on handling life ourselves. Blessed are the arrogant; happy people are ones who depend on themselves. If he wants to give us advice on what to do, we'll be glad to consider it, provided, of course, that he promises to alter things to suit our desires."

God's attitude toward their understanding of things was severe. He rebuked them for speaking harsh words and promised terrible judgment if their attitude didn't change. God had told a much earlier generation of similarly arrogant Hebrews that "no one who has treated me with contempt will ever see [the promised land]" (Num. 14:23). What did he mean?

We treat people with contempt when we do not trust them. When a car salesman states his bottom price, most car buyers smile condescendingly, walk around the car several times, then offer a sum considerably lower. In a sense, that interchange reflects the purchaser's contempt for the salesman. We do not believe what he says; we therefore regard him as an obstacle to get around in pursuit of our best advantage. Depending on our resources to get what we want flows out of a spirit of contempt, and that spirit will keep us from ever finding God.

MARTI AND GRANT

I recently counseled a couple who had been married a little more than ten years. Marti was a clever woman, a clear thinker who quickly cut through to the core of any issue. Her husband, Grant, an insurance salesman, possessed a smooth tongue and a good head for numbers, but he was no intellectual match for his wife.

Early on she recognized that her agile mind threatened him. Wisely or unwisely, she chose to keep her heady thoughts to herself. He fell into the role of genial companion and chatted pleasantly with his wife about everyday things.

After seven years of marriage, Marti began to feel anxious

and depressed. As she struggled to understand her mood shift, she recalled instances of childhood sexual abuse. She asked Grant to come with her to counseling.

It quickly became apparent to me that Grant, faced with Marti's deep pain, was counting on his affability to deal effectively with her. When she would turn to him, sometimes crying, sometimes furious, he smiled and said, "Honey, you're really getting caught up in these things. I know it's tough. Just remember that I love you."

After one especially bland comment that made Marti wince, I suggested to Grant that he seemed uncomfortable with his wife's strong feelings. Angry terror flashed through his eyes. Quickly recovering, he regained the familiar smile, then said, "No, I don't think so. I'm just terribly anxious that Marti feel my love through all this."

"But isn't it true that you were furious at me for just a moment when I suggested that you feel uncomfortable when Marti is upset or mad?"

"I'm disturbed, of course. I don't like seeing my wife hurting. But no, I certainly wasn't angry at you."

"I think you *are* angry," I said. "And I think you're angry because you're depending on the only resource that's ever worked for you—your way with words—to handle this situation with your wife. But her pain requires more of you than tender words. And you're not sure you have what it takes."

I went on. "You've been terrified of your wife for years, partly because of her intelligence and depth. I wonder if the damage done by her sexual abuse isn't nearly so bad as the damage done by your refusal to really engage with her as a man."

He shifted in his chair, looked at me for ten seconds, then lowered his face and said nothing.

"My guess is that right now you're feeling desperate as well as mad. Your major tool for handling people, including your wife, isn't working—and you know it. And you're not sure whether there's anything else within you that you can draw from to respond more meaningfully to Marti."

He lifted his eyes until they met mine. His stare was icy. "I love my wife. I love her well. And I will continue to do so."

With a rage that only terror can provoke, Grant was stiffening in the posture of the fourth floor: "I will survive. And I'll depend on whatever resources I have at my disposal to do it."

Blessed are the arrogant.

FOUR HUNDRED YEARS OF SILENCE

After the Lord rebuked the Jews in Malachi's day for speaking harsh words against him, he closed his mouth for four hundred years. A silence of that length makes you pay attention to whatever breaks it. When God became man four centuries later, his first *official* words to the multitudes were these: "Blessed are the poor in spirit" (Matt. 5:3). The last time he had spoken, he rebuked the Jews for believing that blessedness belongs to the arrogant, to those who think they can manage life on their own. When he came to earth to bring life, he began his work by teaching that happiness comes to those who know they have no ability whatsoever to take care of themselves.

The fallen structure says, "I have what it takes to make it."

The fallen structure says, "I have what it takes to make it. Maybe it's my glib tongue or my agile mind or my great personality. Maybe it's my self-protective retreat into depression or my ability to block out memories; perhaps it's my angry indifference. Maybe it's my ability to make money. I'm a high-energy, creative person. I'll figure out some way to keep my life together. And it will work. *I will survive!*"

Blessed are the arrogant.

THE GODLY STRUCTURE: I WILL OBEY

The godly structure generates a very different attitude: "What I have is utterly insufficient to make my life work. I need more than what I have to relate well to anyone, including a troubled wife. Without God, my resources are worth absolutely nothing. When it comes to currency that can buy life, I'm utterly broke.

"But I know God is good. I know he will supply everything I need to move through any situation in a way that gives me a taste of life and, more important, makes him look good to others. Problems will continue, but I can know God better and reflect him to others, no matter what happens. Knowing my poverty frees me to go after what his currency will purchase.

"Blessed are the poor in spirit. *I will obey.*"

As I write this chapter, I am wrestling with a difficult matter. The ministry to which God has called me is presenting a series of challenges that I am not handling well. Motivation sometimes sags, sleep is often interrupted by worry, and my sense of calling seems less clear.

In the middle of these struggles, my natural tendency is to remind myself of the abilities God has given me and to push forward under the banner of persevering stewardship. When the emotional battle intensifies, I berate myself for having a weak character that can't stand the heat—and I make myself return to the kitchen.

But as I ponder my fallen structure, I am becoming more aware of how stubbornly and fearfully I depend on my talents to win the day. For years, I've been told that I think well. Perhaps my ability to move about in the world of abstract thought has become my god.

Some years back, I fell on concrete, hit my head, and suffered a concussion. For the first half hour in the emergency room, I was delirious. Over and over again, I shouted, "I'll never be able to think again!" Was I mourning the death of my god?

In the current ministry challenges, I am admitting—not without resistance—that my resources may not be enough to move things along toward a favorable outcome. And this admission is freeing me to lay my talents before God to be used as he sees fit. My mind still works—I hope rather well. But the pressure is easing as I learn to require nothing of myself other than to further God's purposes through my life.

The fallen structure is teetering. Praise God! I feel less of a need to try to survive on my own.

Figuring out how to survive on our own is the fifth floor of the fallen structure.

14
Fifth Floor: Here's How
I Will Survive

With the determination to survive comes the requirement to figure out how. More than anything else, we were built to relate. So, quite naturally, the first order of business for fallen people is to develop a strategy for relating to others that will win from them whatever nourishment they can provide and keep us safe from their power to destroy us.

Perhaps nothing reveals more about who we are and how we think about life than how we relate to others. Most of us come up with a fairly consistent plan for getting along with people that hides our weaknesses and parades our strengths. I call that plan a *style of relating*.

When you're with someone long enough, you can usually sense one of two broad patterns of relating. A few folks tune into you with caring intensity. You feel that what you say matters to them. They place all their resources—wisdom, humor, practical skills—at your disposal. They delight to give. Their energy moves toward you.

With most people, the story is disagreeably different. You sense that their jovial friendliness or matter-of-fact efficiency or serious spiritual demeanor has more to do with them than with you. You walk away from them tired, perhaps irritable, and less motivated to do anything important.

A STRING OF COMPLIMENTS

I remember one woman who came to see me professionally when her husband filed for divorce. Within moments of our first meeting, Dana let me know how privileged she felt to have an appointment with me. If I judged by her ceaseless stream of compliments each session, I would conclude that never had I dealt more brilliantly with a client.

During one session, when I suggested that her kind remarks seemed more designed to get me to enjoy her than to encourage me, she smiled sweetly, like a little girl caught doing something wrong but still in control, and said, "You really are clever, aren't you?"

To this day, she still drops me an occasional card that always includes an overdone word of appreciation for the little I've done for her.

Some expressions of warmth spring from a sincere heart and should be gratefully received. Others don't and shouldn't. The difference is in their underlying structure.

Beneath every style of relating, and beneath every conversational exchange, is an energy that reflects either our fallenness or our redemption.* Doubts about God that lead to a self-reliant determination to survive stain our interactions with self-centeredness. As we speak, we may honor agendas that have more to do with our own welfare than the welfare of others.

---

*In every case, of course, there is a mixture of the two structures. No Christian ever operates from a fully fallen base, not even Lot in Sodom, whose grieved heart indicated God was working in him. Neither can a Christian live out of pure godly energy until he sees Christ face to face and is totally persuaded of his goodness.

SHY, SWEET CHRISTINE

In the counseling program I direct, every semester I lead a group of ten students in a weekly two-hour meeting where we think about our styles of relating. When a counselor's pattern of interacting builds on a fallen structure, it interferes with her efforts to help.

In one such group meeting, Christine, a tall, attractive blonde-haired woman, said very little. In our tenth meeting, another member of the group, Eva, a feisty brunette, asked Christine why she didn't participate more.

"Oh, I really don't have much to say," Christine answered with a demure smile. "And I enjoy listening to each of you. But I'll be happy to reply to anything you'd like to ask."

I quickly turned to Eva and asked her how that comment made her feel.

"Dismissed. Put off. I can't imagine that she would ever want to really talk with me. It's like she won't allow any of us to get close to her."

I then turned to Christine. "Does that reaction make sense to you? It's pretty much what I felt, too. Your smile and your choice of words tell me that you have no intention of ever letting us get to know you. I wonder if you see yourself as a person who intends to stay very much in control."

Several weeks later, Christine admitted to the group, "I never give myself to anyone. I always play it safe. I have to. My dad left home when I was little, and I became my mother's prize. She always dressed me in overly cute clothes. I felt like a model sent out to display mother's latest designs.

"I can remember deciding that I would never let anyone get to know the real me, that I would use a shy sort of sweetness to keep people at a distance, like I did when mother displayed me to her friends. You don't know how much I hate being sweet. But I've been terrified to be anything else. I've never felt worth knowing."

Within the context of this group, Christine eventually

acknowledged her arrogance, her anger at God and others, and her terror of facing life alone.

THE GODLY STRUCTURE: HERE'S HOW I WILL LIVE

How would Christine relate if she were living in the energy of a godly structure? Suppose she believed that God was good, despite an abandoning father and a possessive mother. Suppose she understood that his goodness is most fully revealed at the cross, where God solved her biggest problem. Suppose she turned to people to give them something for their sake, trusting that because of God's work in her she had something to give. Suppose she continued to long for people's maturity and joy even when they mistreated her, and she judged her own failure to love with the humble but cheerful grace of someone already forgiven. And, finally, suppose she moved into life eager to obey rather than determined to survive.

The godly structure begins with trusting and loving God, and it ends by freeing us to love people with all the beauty and richness of our unique identities.

Then, among other things, she might talk more in a group, and she wouldn't be as sweet. She would be sensitive to her influence on others, not because she wanted to protect herself or keep others happy with her, but because she would sincerely want to encourage them. She might argue a little more and speak up when she saw something wrong. Some sweetness would remain; only now it would be genuine. And others would know it and be blessed. Her style of relating would change.

Nothing matters more than how we relate to God and to others. The fallen structure begins with doubting God, then hating him, and ends with using people, protecting ourselves from them, and leading unreleased lives, with the good that God has placed within us safely tucked away beneath self-centered efforts to avoid pain. The godly structure begins with trusting and loving God, and it ends by freeing us to love people with all the beauty and richness of our unique identities.

Both the fallen structure and the godly structure we've been discussing are summarized in the diagrams on the following pages.

Now comes the big question: How do we make the shift from a fallen structure to a godly one? If we are to find God, we must seek him with all our heart. We cannot do that with the fallen structure in place. It must be dismantled. Something within us must be *disrupted* and something from outside must *entice* us to walk a path that leads to God. Disruption and enticement are the work of God's Spirit. Our work is to invite him to do *his*.

THE FALLEN STRUCTURE

PROBLEMS IN LIVING

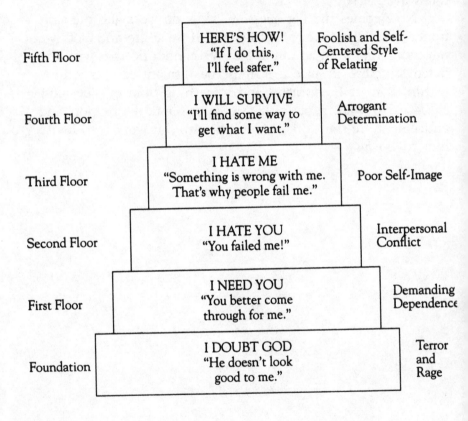

Fifth Floor	**HERE'S HOW!** "If I do this, I'll feel safer."	Foolish and Self-Centered Style of Relating
Fourth Floor	**I WILL SURVIVE** "I'll find some way to get what I want."	Arrogant Determination
Third Floor	**I HATE ME** "Something is wrong with me. That's why people fail me."	Poor Self-Image
Second Floor	**I HATE YOU** "You failed me!"	Interpersonal Conflict
First Floor	**I NEED YOU** "You better come through for me."	Demanding Dependence
Foundation	**I DOUBT GOD** "He doesn't look good to me."	Terror and Rage

THE GODLY STRUCTURE

FRUITFUL LIVING

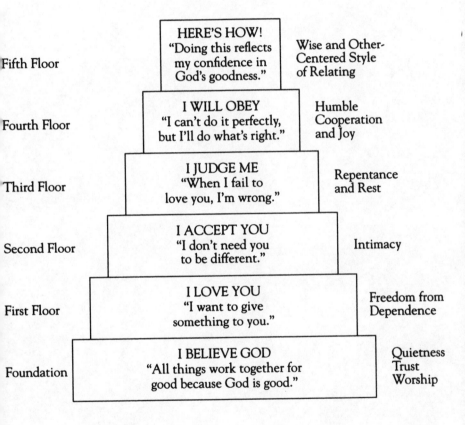

Fifth Floor — HERE'S HOW! "Doing this reflects my confidence in God's goodness." — Wise and Other-Centered Style of Relating

Fourth Floor — I WILL OBEY "I can't do it perfectly, but I'll do what's right." — Humble Cooperation and Joy

Third Floor — I JUDGE ME "When I fail to love you, I'm wrong." — Repentance and Rest

Second Floor — I ACCEPT YOU "I don't need you to be different." — Intimacy

First Floor — I LOVE YOU "I want to give something to you." — Freedom from Dependence

Foundation — I BELIEVE GOD "All things work together for good because God is good." — Quietness Trust Worship

III
THE PATHWAY TO
FINDING GOD

15
Darkness Before Light

I want to set the tone for these closing chapters by giving the highlights of a recent entry from the journal I keep sporadically. The tone may sound negative, overly gloomy, morbid. But suffering comes before laughter, the pain of birth precedes the wonder of new life, and questions must be asked before confidence develops. Disillusionment is the soil in which hope grows. The Spirit of God must first disrupt something bad within us before he entices us with the promise of joy. I wrote the journal entry in the summer of 1992 during a three-hour plane trip. As I arrived at the airport, I became aware of a crushing sadness within me that utterly eliminated any experience of joy or hope. Spiritual fruit seemed entirely absent.

I include this personal disclosure of a hard time because my experience, I think, is not uncommon. Honest people, stained by sin and tortured by hope for what seems beyond reach, walk through deep valleys. I offer the following highlights in the hope that it might strengthen someone's faith enough to outlast his or her trial. The road to finding God takes us through darkness before it brings us to light.

JOURNAL ENTRY: JULY 1, 1992

Sometimes my soul feels dead. Other times tortured. Right now I feel a terrible combination of both.

I hate these times. I wish I were a simple, happy man. I know people who seem so much happier than I. Why must I go through these bouts with despair? When I do, I have trouble finding within me—or in anyone else—something that brings joy. I am utterly miserable, a terrible advertisement for Christianity. I wonder if people who read my books imagine that I can get this low.

During these times of anguish, I am genuinely afraid. I feel it right now. Is there enough left of me to continue on, to do my work, to love my family, to face life? Or have I disappeared into a cave of dark, tangled tunnels, a cold black maze that angles downward from which I will never emerge?

I am utterly miserable, a terrible advertisement for Christianity.

I worry, but not with a productive frenzy that gets me moving. My worry feels more like despair, like falling into that black hole and wondering whether the next bump will be the final one that kills me or merely one more crash against the wall before I hit bottom.

What can I do? I can't stand feeling this way. I'm no good to anyone like this. Where's God? What's he supposed to be doing? I want to move, to choose something aggressively. But a deep, angry boredom, a hopeless indifference, has robbed me of energy. I can't run, walk, or stand. At best, I seem only to shuffle along the path of least resistance, pouting more than grumbling.

But if I continue to shuffle, merely to drift with the tide, I fear losing my mind. I long to become a mature, stable, loving man, someone my wife can draw strength from and enjoy. I *must* not drift. I *must* take action.

But that's the problem. The idea of moving presupposes an energy within me capable of being harnessed. It assumes that I exist as a real, separate entity, as someone who is able to choose a direction freely and then follow it.

Taking action presumes something further—a reason to move this way and not that, a benevolent Creator behind this whole mess with a good design that I might miss if I ignore him.

To move at all, I must believe these two things: one, that I exist beneath my pain as a free person who can move, and, two, that there really is an infinitely good Person who invites me to move toward a joy that he provides.

If I believe that God is good and I am free, then I can move through the ups and downs of life with hope—there is meaning to be found. Goodness is greater than badness. There's reason for cheer.

Someone is there! Final reality is personal. I know it.

If, however, I believe in only one or neither, then life is a hopeless tragedy, a cruel hoax, enticing me toward something it cannot provide. It becomes a mockery, laughing at me, hatefully sneering at my every effort to rise above its pointlessness—or to retreat from it. I am then left with nothing but pain, unending and unendurable.

But even as I write, I cannot help but notice two things— and I smell hope. When I speak of unbelief, I still think of final reality as more than an "it." I just spoke of "it" mocking me. But *things* aren't capable of mockery. Only *persons* are. Matter mocks no one. Matter simply is. Only persons mock. Persons mock—or love—other persons. Laughing at a strange rock formation or a silly-looking dog is entirely different from laughing at a friend. I believe God exists. And I believe I exist.

I can't get away from the idea of a personal energy outside of myself big enough to hem me in. I can think of this personal reality as good or bad, but I can't envision his (not "its") absence, his nonexistence.

Someone is there! Final reality is personal. I know it. It must be. The inconsolable longings within me, to say nothing of the intricate design of an insect, can be explained in no other way. The question then becomes: Is this Final Person good or bad?

And that question drives me to my second observation. Not only do I reflexively think of a Person beyond matter, but I also envision that Person moving toward me and feeling something for me as he comes closer.

I find that I cannot break away from a bedrock fact: *reality is defined by the interaction of two persons,* one, an infinite Person who is either good or bad; and two, me, and a community of people just like me, individuals who are free to move away from or toward the infinite Person depending on what we believe about him.

What do I believe about him? I know I exist and I know he exists. But is he good, and therefore worthy of trust and a legitimate basis of hope? Or is he bad, and am I therefore alone, abandoned to my resources to find happiness in a world that doesn't have it to give, unless I pretend I want less than I know I want.

When I push matters that far, I discover within me a strangely unshakable conviction that this Ultimate Person is, in fact, the God of the Bible, the God revealed in Jesus Christ, someone thoroughly good, relentlessly moral, unstoppably powerful, unimaginably loving, and determined to display his highest virtues by making me extremely happy.

If I make myself ask why I believe God is good, why the Supreme Being is not bad, my attention goes quickly to my thirst for beauty: the beauty of love, the beauty of order, the beauty of joy. I know the lust for beauty is within me—I can't get away from it. And I know it is a *good* lust, one that I can deny but never eliminate. If beauty has no source, I don't know how to explain my desire for it.

I find myself being brought to a foundation that I cannot

fall beneath. There is a God and he is good. And I am alive as a person with the capacity to trust him or turn away from him.

Now I can see the final reality of a relational encounter between God and me for what it really is. The question to ask is not, "What will I do with God?" but rather, "What will he do with me, someone who refuses to trust his goodness?"

The moment I ask that question with the urgency it deserves, something happens. It is then that I catch a glimpse of God's blazing glory. What has he done with me? He accepts me! He loves me! That glimpse gives me a taste of him, and I know that he is good beyond every imagination.

He sees my rebellion, my refusal to trust him, my determination to build my city here. He also sees how easily my feeble desire to do what is good is overwhelmed by stronger desires for bad things. And still he loves me! He feels compassion toward me! He wants me for a friend!

As I ponder the relationship between God and me—one that he has arranged—I sense the stirrings of hope. I see light. The cave is still black, but I am no longer falling more deeply into it. Through no power of mine, I feel myself being lifted out of it. I find myself walking in a meadow blooming with wild flowers, moving toward a stream of clear water, then lying down beside it on a grassy bank.

The sun is shining, warming my body, while a gentle breeze keeps me from becoming uncomfortably hot. And I am aware of the sheer joy of being alive. I seem to be resting and moving at the same time, resting in Christ and moving toward him, farther and farther away from the black hole that so recently had been my prison. And I think I shall never fall into that hole again.

Then something happens, perhaps small, perhaps big. A filling falls out of a tooth. I receive disturbing news about someone I love. I struggle to maintain perspective, but it slips away. I tell myself that God is still good, that I can trust him, but the reality is gone. In an instant, the grassy bank disappears, and I am again plummeting into darkness. Again my soul feels dead, tortured, alive only with pain and doubt.

The cycle repeats itself, this time with lower lows and higher highs. I'm pressed again to return to my foundations: Is God really good? Do I believe it? Am I alive with the power to pursue him? Is he still there? Will he let me find him? I become more aware of the importance of trusting him, of resting in his goodness, of choosing against sin.

Sometimes I wish I could settle for merely engaging pleasantly with life, brushing my teeth, paying my bills, and correcting my slice off the tee. But the pursuit of God requires more.

The more I see the real issues of life, the more I have no choice but to move toward spiritual greatness or spiritual failure, toward powerful depth or bland impotence. I long to become a man of God, to know Christ well enough for him to be recognizable in me through my moody, fickle weirdness. I want him; sometimes I want him more than life itself. I must seek him with all my heart; only then will he let me find him. And only if I find him will I know the joy of living.

Lord, another glimpse, please!

(End of journal entry.)

UNDERMINING OUR FALLEN STRUCTURE

We will glimpse God when our fallen structure is undermined and we are enticed to pursue God as the final good in our lives. For that to occur, we must have the courage to do three things.

First, we must *face our impact on people.* When we see how we harm those we love, our redeemed hearts suffer to the point of repentance. When our impact is good, we sense a joy that makes us long to love even better.

Second, we must *face the damage done to us by other people.* When we honestly acknowledge how others have failed us, we begin to see how hard we work to avoid further injury by withholding from others whatever makes us feel vulnerable. Such withholding generates a longing within us to exist more fully with all that we are, to give our tenderness to others who may trample it underfoot, to move more strongly even though we may fail.

Third, we must *face our attitude toward God*. It seems that God has failed us. We do not fully trust him. At times we feel enraged by him. As we admit how we think about God, we feel jarred. Something clearly is not right. A passion arises within us to trust him, to experience him as the good God he claims to be, to rest peacefully in the knowledge that he is thoroughly good and always there for us.

We must learn to tell the story of our lives—how we impact others, how we've been damaged by others, how we feel about God—in order to disrupt the sinful attitudes and practices that still remain. Telling our stories requires us to face painful truths about ourselves. And once we've faced those truths, we will again feel the noble passions to love, to be, and to worship, passions planted in our hearts by God's Spirit.

Too often, however, we avoid the ugly details of our story, or we obsessively explore them. Neither will lead us toward finding God.

16
Mistakes People Make

We find God by developing a confidence in his character that frees us to rest, to stop struggling to make life work as we want it to, to no longer demand specific proofs of his goodness. But in a world where the evidence of his kindness is obscured by so much pain and uncertainty, developing that confidence is not easy.

In trying to find God, we often make one of two mistakes.

MOVING AROUND OUR PROBLEMS

First, we move *around* our problems to restore our confidence that God is good. Telling a man struggling with homosexual urges or a woman battling bulimia to engage in more God-centered activities is going around their problems. Spending more time in Bible study and dropping to our knees more frequently in prayer sometimes helps us avoid the very realities of life that, if faced, could meaningfully drive us to God.

We will not find God by detaching ourselves from the ugly, painful realities of the world around us or within us. When we refuse to own all that is happening in our lives, when we never "tell our stories" to one another, our pursuit of God is reduced to an organized set of activities energized only by the proud passion of discipline.

A seminary student came to me for help with his problem of masturbation. I asked him to tell me how he related to other people. I suspected that his chronic yielding to sexual temptation was strengthened by an approach to people that robbed him of the legitimate joys of masculine involvement. If he either dominated others (counterfeit masculinity) or easily capitulated to them (absent masculinity), then the core of his male soul would feel empty. That emptiness would then drive him to find the fullness he was intended to enjoy, but until his unmasculine style of relating changed, he would be especially drawn to an experience of instant fullness that required no risk. To overcome his compulsive masturbation, he would need to move toward others with the compassionate courage of manhood.

When I asked him to describe his relational patterns, I expected to find self-protective patterns of relating: either dominating others or retreating from them.

He immediately replied, "Just as I thought! You want to explore my psychological insides to provide me with an excuse for my sin. What you should have done was direct me to Scriptures that exhort self-control and condemn masturbation as a sinful means of relieving sexual energy."

The route to God never takes us around our problems.

I later learned he was part of a group that wanted to expose me as an unbiblical counselor. For him, *biblical counseling meant never looking at our lives beyond obvious sins of behavior. He wanted to move around* the problems in his life to find God through increased discipline in moral living.

We must learn to tell the story of our lives—the good, the bad, and the ugly—to explore who we are: twisted image-bearers who live together in a community of other twisted image-bearers in the presence of an untwisted God, who is slowly making us straight. We will never find God by denying who we are and where we've been. The route to God never takes us around our problems.

GETTING ABSORBED IN OUR PROBLEMS

Neither will we find God by *absorbing* ourselves in our problems. That's mistake number two. The modern counseling movement sometimes encourages us to walk down this blind alley. Rather than going around our problems, we are told to move into them, to face them fully, to pretend about nothing. Denial becomes the supreme vice; honesty and openness, the greatest virtues.

Patti struggled with insecurity. As a result, she cooperated with everyone's plans but her own. She was exhausted, full of self-contempt, and severely depressed. Her recovery group encouraged her to establish clearer boundaries, to say no more frequently, and to do more often what she wanted to do. But she couldn't find the courage to follow their counsel. Someone in the group recommended individual therapy.

For ten months, Patti spent one hour per week exploring every wound she had suffered, every disappointment she had felt, every scar that bore evidence of mistreatment. When she defended her father as someone "who tried to love me; he just didn't know how," her therapist insisted she face what a wicked man he was and how deeply she hated him. Her background in a conservative church was exposed as "toxic," persuading her that she was sinful but offering little grace. Memories of sexual abuse by her youth pastor surfaced. She was encouraged to feel the depths of that trauma.

The message of therapy was that lifting denial would free

her to express all that she felt, and that complete self-expression was the necessary foundation of restored joy.

Like most errors, this one begins with a truth and pushes it too far. We must not move around our problems; we must *move into* them if we are to find God. But our problems can be so fascinating, and facing them so enlivening, that we can easily become absorbed in them. We have lost the balance. Christian self-help books explain what is happening in us and outline methods for repairing what's wrong far better than they present the wonders of life in Christ.

We have lost the idea that ongoing struggles with such things as low self-esteem and loneliness may be God's means of drawing us into a closer relationship with him.

The effect of this second error is that we face our problems *too much*; we get bogged down in them and never go *through* them. We have lost the idea that ongoing struggles with such things as low self-esteem, scars from sexual abuse, and loneliness may be God's means of drawing us into a closer relationship with him. Our thinking runs along these lines: "I cannot love others until I first love myself. Working on self-acceptance must be my top priority. I will trust God to heal my damaged sense of identity and when he does, *then* I will serve him. But I cannot move *through* my problems to worry about anyone else until those problems are resolved, no more than a runner can enter a race until his broken leg is healed." Such thinking causes us to become mired in our problems, absorbed by them with a selfish energy that masquerades as a commitment to personal growth.

MOVING THROUGH OUR PROBLEMS

We will walk a very different path if we move *through* our problems to find God rather than *around* them in denial or *into* them to the point of absorption. My purpose in this final section of the book is to point us toward the pathway through our problems toward God.

17
Our Good Passions
Are Too Weak

We find God to the degree that we *want* to find him. Until our passion for finding God exceeds all other passions, and until we long to know him as our Lord and friend more than to use him to get what we want (the way a spoiled child uses a rich father), we will not find him as deeply as he longs to be found. He will not reveal himself to us in those wonderful glimpses of his love or in that quiet reassurance that he is with us.

God wants to let us find him. Especially when years of living as a Christian have seemingly brought us no closer to him, God delights to be discovered. He is not playing hard to get. Something about the way we are and who he is makes it necessary for us to want him more than we want anyone or anything else before we can find him. "'You will seek me and find me when you seek me with all your heart. I will be found by you,' declares the LORD" (Jer. 29:13–14).

Developing this kind of passion is not easy. Getting up a half hour earlier to spend time with God will help, but it won't get the job done. Our desires, even for God, are so badly corrupted with self-centeredness that they cannot be purified by personal discipline, religious activity, or enthusiastic singing.

NEGOTIATING WITH GOD

Too often, we demand that God demonstrate his goodness in a specific way. Peter once asked Jesus, "We have left everything to follow you! What then will there be for us?" (Matt. 19:27).

We find God to the degree that we want to find him.

The Lord replied to Peter's question by telling a story of workers in a vineyard. A landowner hired some men to work all day in his vineyard for the usual daily wage. Later in the day, he hired other workers, saying, "I will pay you whatever is right." When, at the end of the day, he paid all the workers the same whether they had worked one hour or twelve hours, those who had worked all day grumbled. The landowner replied, "I am not being unfair to you. Didn't you agree to work for a denarius? Take your pay and go. . . . Don't I have the right to do what I want with my own money?"

This story highlights the need for servants to trust their master to do what is right. Like Peter, we commonly talk about trust, but we practice negotiation. We come to God believing that he rewards those who earnestly seek him, but then insist that we be rewarded right away with what we think we deserve.

The seeking that gets rewarded, however, allows no spirit of negotiation. It is a trusting passion that emboldens us to ask for everything our hearts desire, like children before Christmas, but at the same time frees us to remain deeply content with whatever comes.

STRENGTHENING GOOD PASSIONS

When the subject of passion comes up, most of us immediately think of strong desires within us that we wish weren't there. The enemy has become dark desires—lust, worry, anger, and the like—and the power of the enemy, we assume, is the self-hatred and shame we've learned in dysfunctional communities.

To resist these desires—to stop drinking, to stop buying pornography, to stop losing our tempers—we think we must first weaken them. They feel so powerful that when we're in the grips of them, they seem irresistible. And so we try to understand them in a way that makes them less appealing and to draw power from sources outside ourselves that will enable us to resist them. We work to weaken bad passions.

---

*The core problem is not that we are
too passionate about bad things,
but that we are not passionate enough
about good things.*

But perhaps *bad passions are strong because good passions are weak.* Maybe the problem is not too much desire, but rather too little. The core problem with most of us, including the sex addict, the workaholic, and the victim of childhood abuse, is not that we are too passionate about bad things, but that we are not passionate enough about good things.

We will not overcome our addictions by looking for ways to weaken them or by focusing on our need for power to resist them. Uncovering the roots of homosexual urges in the hopes of reducing their intensity will not, in the long run, prove helpful. And drawing strength from one's community simply creates another addiction, this one to the community.

Something must be released within us that *wants* to resist more than to yield. We must become caught up in a larger, compelling purpose that strengthens good passions. When holiness becomes more attractive than sin, when knowing God seems more important than finding self, when no cost seems too great to pay for the privilege of intimacy with Christ, then we will find the strength to resist sin meaningfully—not perfectly, but meaningfully. Then our obedience will be sincere rather than manipulative. Then our efforts to live properly will seem more like *going after* something good than *giving up* something good.

Our Lord promised to reveal himself to people who demonstrate their love by obeying him (John 14:21). We must obey if we are to experience Christ in our lives. But this obedience is never a chore; it's a delight, a privilege, a response to the deepest passions of the heart. To those who walk the path of glad obedience Christ reveals himself in blazing glimpses that cast a shadow on every lesser desire.

GROUND BEEF VERSUS FILET MIGNON

But for most of us, Christ is in the shadow, and something else shines more brightly. That despicable fallen structure within us—our tendency to doubt God's goodness—has dulled our appetite for what is good. The energy of a self-reliant spirit has cut the deepest nerve endings of our souls, leaving us bored with those things that could bring the richest joys and addictively caught up with lesser, and often sinful, pleasures.

We are more flattered by an invitation to an exclusive party than we are by the opportunity to pray. We find more delight in being wanted by certain people than in being accepted by God. The loss of respect from friends hurts more than loss of fellowship with Christ. Getting a better paying job is more exciting than seeing God work through us to encourage someone else.

Something is dreadfully wrong. The situation is like someone whose taste buds salivate at the mention of ground beef but register nothing when filet mignon is offered.

The loss of appetite for the good things God designed us to enjoy is the most tragic evidence of the fallen structure within us. The joy of giving has been replaced by the pleasure of getting. The thrill of living as unthreatened people who can continue to give no matter how we're treated stirs us less than the chance to protect ourselves against assaults on our dignity and to affirm our value in the midst of a demeaning world. And the sheer excitement of standing fully accepted in the presence of God is less appealing than straightening out our lives. Rather than finding God, we prefer to relieve our terror of life by making money and friends, and we express our rage at a God who cannot be trusted by arrogantly trusting ourselves.

Responsible living, we assume, obligates God to keep blessing us.

Somehow we have killed the passion that should be strongest and are ruled by weaker passions.

A husband and wife get into a fight. What matters most to them in the middle of it? Finding God and reflecting his character to the other? Or proving a point, relieving tension, or figuring out how to correct what went wrong?

Parents discover that their teenage son has been smoking marijuana. Where do their minds immediately go? Do they trust the Lord and move toward their son in the strength of that trust? Or do they castigate themselves for failing as parents and immediately come up with a game plan for getting him away from bad influences?

A woman falls into a depression so severe that she enjoys nothing. What purpose governs her behavior? Finding God to continue serving him no matter how bad she feels? Or finding a doctor who can relieve the depression with medication or therapy?

Why is our appetite for God so much weaker than our appetite for solutions to life's problems? If God is as good as he claims to be and if our souls' richest pleasure depends on knowing him, our first thought in every situation ought to be to find him. But it isn't.

A PLAN TO FOLLOW

Nothing makes us lose a proper focus more quickly than pain, and nothing keeps us from recognizing a wrong focus more than a life that is going well. We think the blessings should continue, especially if we keep doing our part. Responsible living, we assume, obligates God to keep blessing us.

When our strongest passion is to solve our problems, we look for a *plan to follow* rather than *a person to trust*. We study the Bible, read Christian books, attend seminars, and listen to sermons to discover a plan that will produce results. Like the ancients who examined the movements of the stars to discover their destiny (and then hopefully do something about it), we ask God to unroll the blueprints for a better life, and then we hire a specialist to help us interpret them.

But honest people who have lived a while wonder whether any plan works. They notice more and more evidence that tells them the usual formulas just don't produce, not even the Christian ones. What they assumed were promises from God aren't kept. Communication techniques taught at a Christian seminar on relationships don't relieve all marital tensions, and carefully following biblical principles of financial stewardship doesn't always solve all money problems.

There are no guarantees that life will work as we want. God gives us biblical principles not so that we can arrange our lives according to our taste, but so that we can know how God wants us to live. What happens in our lives when we live as he directs is up to God. Sometimes the blessings come. Sometimes they don't. Only when we lose hope in formulas that guarantee success will we develop true hope in a God who can be trusted when life makes no sense, because one day he'll take us home.

TRUST IN AN ORDERLY WORLD

We can approach life in two ways: *either* live with a confidence in an orderly world and try to manage things ourselves, *or* face life's tragedy and chaos and develop confidence in someone bigger than the chaos, someone whose goodness overwhelms tragedy, someone who cares about us.

Trust in an orderly world dies hard. We are terrified of being vulnerable. We demand control over those things that matter most: our children, our important relationships, our health, our bank accounts. We angrily refuse to believe that life is more chaotic than it is predictable; we don't want to believe that the only way to survive with joy is to trust someone stronger than ourselves.

---

*Our primary purpose is not to use God
to solve problems but to move through
our problems toward finding God.*

And when life goes as we desire, it is nearly impossible to resist a subtle form of pride: "There's an order to life, and I have found it and followed it. I praise God that I'm not like others who simply won't live as they should." Parents of adult children who have turned out well may look condescendingly at parents whose unmarried daughter is pregnant.

Shattered dreams, however, provide a unique opportunity to change our minds about the predictability of life. When sincere efforts to do right do not produce the blessings we expect, we lose confidence in a manageable order. Sometimes, of course, we blame ourselves for not following God's plan as well as we should have, but even in the middle of self-contempt, we begin to realize that good living does not guarantee desired blessing.

And we should nurture that thought. Living responsibly, though important, should not be our top priority in life. Life will not always reward good performance. Things are not that predictable. When unexpected problems develop that cannot be explained by earlier failure, we lose confidence in our ability to keep our lives together. We sink in a deep mire where trust in God is our only option. Perhaps that explains why true passion for God grows best in the dark.

OUR PRIMARY PURPOSE

Nothing matters more than developing a passion for Christ as we try to handle life's struggles responsibly and wisely. Our primary purpose is not to use God to solve problems but to move through our problems toward finding God. We must develop a confidence in God that keeps us going even when hard problems continue. And that confidence develops only when confidence in our strategies to make life work is shattered. For that reason we can welcome ongoing difficulties that make us question our ability to avoid or overcome them.

God is ashamed to be known as the God of people who devote their energies to building a satisfying life in this world, who take lightly the promise of a better country, and who live for the present. He is *not* ashamed, however, to be called the God of people who enjoy legitimate pleasures now but who clearly refuse to build their cities here; who look forward to a better home in another land; who are willing to feel the ache of unsatisfied longings without making any demands for relief; and who are grateful for the chance to serve God in an unfriendly world until they find their rest in an eternal city. (See Hebrews 11, particularly verses 13–16.)

Our passion for finding God is too weak. God reveals himself to people who want to know him more than they want anything else. As we struggle through the problems of life, the most important question we can ask is not, "How can I solve my problems?" but rather, "How can I develop a burning passion for knowing Christ that will overwhelm all other passions and reduce them to secondary concerns?"

18
The Nature of Good and Bad Passions: Toward Disrupting the Bad and Releasing the Good

We must recover our passion for God—or we will never really live. The church will continue to be filled with proper, moral Christians who sense little of the excitement of contact with the supernatural and whose lives are unattractively different from non-Christians. Passion for God must be restored—but how? What can we do to move God to reveal himself more fully to us until we are consumed with Christ?

God does no deeper work in a person's soul than to stir a passion for finding him that exceeds all other passions. If we can understand how to cooperate with the Spirit's development of that passion, when problems hit we will be better prepared to move through those problems toward finding God.

We need to find a direction to take that will *disrupt the bad passions* that too often rule us and *release the good passions* lying dormant within us. To follow this direction with wisdom and to resist the tendency to reduce it to a guaranteed formula that obligates God to do what we expect, we must understand the nature of good and bad passions. Let me organize my thoughts into four points.

1. Bad passions run deep.

Bad passions are firmly anchored in the fallen way we approach life, and they are easily triggered. Therefore we spend most of our lives battling against bad passions or giving in to them. In either case, they rule us.

The smallest trigger can arouse violently strong feelings. A spouse's disdainful glance or a derisive edge in someone's voice may instantly enrage us or fill us with fear and self-hatred. Terrible emotions explode within us, seemingly out of nowhere. And when they come, they feel irresistible. They take over our lives and rule us like a hated tyrant.

We seethe with resentment, boil with jealousy, and burn with lust. We despise these feelings, but strangely, at the same time, we find ways to nourish them. To others, we present a facade that things are just fine even while the hatred boils within us. We don't know what else to do.

Then we happen upon a pattern of behavior that relieves the turmoil and fills us, for one golden moment, with a wonderful sense of completion and rest and satisfaction. We may win recognition for exceptional performance in school, on the athletic field, in a church youth group, or on a dance floor. We may masturbate for the first time while staring at pornography. Or we may eat that second dessert to hide our anger at a spouse.

A flush of joy comes over us. Everything comes together in an experience we mistake for life. We feel alive, happy with fulfillment, invigorated with power, liberated to be ourselves, comforted by pleasure, and secure in the reliability of control. That pattern becomes the source of everything good. We depend on it for relief from the nagging pain that never entirely quits.

Over the years, however, that pattern becomes more and more consuming. We feel driven to succeed, or we develop a sexual addiction, or we sacrifice relationships to honor our urge to overeat. In our determination to recover a sense of aliveness, we avoid anything threatening. To do so, some folks (usually those who have been severely abused) fragment their identity into several distinct personalities, each one created to preserve something of who they are in the presence of terrible, destructive pain. The pattern that once brought life (or at least what seemed like life) may mature into deviant sexual expression, the lifeless practice of disciplined religion, a never-satisfied need to be perfect, or a severe emotional disorder.

At some point, we identify the pattern as a problem. It no longer works as it once did. We know something is wrong. We ask for help. And our purpose in getting help is typically to overcome whatever problem interferes with our happiness. "If only I could control my perverted sexual urges" or "If only I felt better about myself" or "If only I didn't feel so tired all the time"—*then* life could be good!

We commit ourselves to solving our problems and to using all available resources (including God) to get the job done. This commitment keeps us preoccupied with something other than finding God. Rather than indulging in patterns of living that create problems, we begin to search for patterns of living that overcome problems. But at heart we are still preoccupied with ourselves; we are more passionately determined to enjoy life than to know better the One who *is* life. We have not disrupted the fallen structure; we have simply substituted one wrong passion for another.

We are more passionately determined to enjoy life than to know better the One who is life.

The fruit of the fallen structure is any *ruling passion* that directs us to look for life in anything other than knowing Christ better by obeying him more completely. The fruit of the godly structure is radically different. When God's Spirit is having his way with us, *noble passions* are released within us that draw us to the source of everything good.

Because we doubt God's goodness, we permit ourselves to desire only what we can control. Sexual pleasures, for example, substitute for the joys of lovingly and nondefensively giving ourselves to one another.

We will be ruled by bad passions until we develop confidence in God's goodness. Our doubts must yield to faith. We must do something to disrupt these bad passions that have us so firmly in their grip. Bad passions run deep. That's my first point. My second point is more encouraging.

2. Noble passions lie dormant in every Christian, waiting to be released.

Every redeemed heart has the urge to see others become whole, the desire to become more in order to give more, and the passion to worship someone strong and good. But our noble passions are smothered under our determination to make it through life without fully trusting God. We try to find ways to make ourselves whole, assert ourselves, and achieve our goals. The effect, of course, is to keep potentially noble passions in hibernation.

But they are still there, asleep perhaps, but not gone. The capacity to long deeply for the good things that draw us to God cannot be destroyed in a heart invaded by God's Spirit; but it can be suppressed. Let me illustrate with a story.

Teri had been married for five years. She always closed her eyes when her husband made love to her. Years of childhood abuse had destroyed all hope that anyone could meaningfully love her. Closing her eyes protected her from seeing any hint of selfish lust in her husband when he approached her sexually. She could accept his advances if she blocked out how deeply she longed for a gentle purity in his love.

At one point during our work together, I asked her to look

into her husband's eyes the next time he kissed her. She gasped in terror and said, "You're asking too much!"

"Think what you most want to see happen in your relationship," I replied. "You certainly want something more than never to reexperience the pain of abuse. You want to be loved well and to love well. You long to be a warm, secure woman who is appreciated by a husband who feels deeply encouraged by his wife. Closing your eyes shuts out not only what you fear but also how bad you want something good. Every time you close your eyes, you are shutting out the possibility of enjoying God as worthy of your trust, and you are missing the opportunity to make your husband really happy by fully giving yourself to him."

Later she told me that opening her eyes during a kiss was the most terrifying and wonderful experience of her life—until she opened them during sexual intercourse. That moment was even more terrifying, but it contained the potential for even deeper excitement.

Because we lack confidence in God, we pretend that the deepest longings of our heart (to be good like God) do not really exist and that far less noble satisfactions can make us happy. We fight against the good passions because, when we don't trust God, they make us miserable. We need a different option: we need to feel those passions that drive us either to the agony of despair or the settled thrill of trust.

Noble passions are rarely aroused, but sometimes we think they are when they're not. And that brings me to my third point.

3. Bad passions can disguise themselves as good ones.

A husband who has tried all he knows to warm up a cold marriage may retreat behind a banner of nondemanding patience when he fails. "I just don't know what's wrong with her. I've done everything I can. All that's left is prayer." But love like Christ's, which is truly noble passion, never quits. It stops at nothing, including the risk of terrible conflict, to reveal itself to one who rejects it.

Lonely people who eat too much may feel nobly defeated by their compulsive hunger: "Something stronger than me is driving me to eat. Just making it through one meal without overeating is worthy of applause." It is natural to find comfort in good intentions or to see ourselves as victimized by urges over which we have no control. But when the apostle Paul felt the urge to do things he really didn't want to do, he didn't look for a way to bolster his self-esteem. He rather declared himself wretched and turned to God for forgiving and enabling grace (Rom. 7:24–25).

A conscious decision to please God (by rearing our children in love, moving toward unresponsive spouses, and determining to lose weight) is only the first step on the path to becoming ruled by good passion. And as the journey progresses and we become increasingly ruled by good passion, we may feel the strength of bad passions more than when we were ruled by them. And that's my final point.

4. Bad passions are often more sensual, but noble passions are more appealing.

We may be *ruled* by a passion for God but *feel* bad passions with a stronger intensity. The measure of what rules us is not which passions *feel* stronger but rather which passions we are *obeying.*

We should not judge ourselves too harshly when lust and jealousy feel stronger than our passion to know God. The pleasures of sin are immediately sensual, and they block out pain. The enjoyment of God increases slowly over time, and is regularly accompanied by suffering. Sensual joy (do I feel good?) is not a reliable measure of whether our lifestyle is godly. Maturing people are sometimes miserable (Hos. 5:15).

> *The measure of what rules us is not which passions feel stronger but rather which passions we are obeying.*

Biblical metaphors—*panting* after God, *tasting* God, *drinking* living water, *eating* bread from heaven—make it clear that finding God is not merely academic. We are to do more than understand truth about God; we are to encounter him, as a bride encounters her husband on their wedding night. Finding God is a sensual experience.

But until we actually see Christ, our natural appetites and fears may seem more urgent and compelling. When we lose sleep over job worries, we shouldn't feel guilty—provided we refuse to make relief from anxiety and insomnia our first priority.

Life can be tough. And godly people will feel its impact. But we are not to depend on sinful measures, like immoral fantasies, to calm our nerves.

When bad passions seem to have the upper hand, we must remind ourselves that God is working to entice us with the prospect of knowing him, and he is appealing to parts of our souls that are not drawn to lesser pleasures. And those parts define who we really are as Christians.

God's method of drawing us closer to him is to disrupt the fallen structure by allowing us to feel the terror and pain the structure was designed to overcome. He then entices us with the hope of finding in him the satisfaction of every noble desire.

God disrupts and entices us, revealing his wrath against sin and his trustworthy goodness, by moving through us *as we live our lives.* He does not ask us to scrub ourselves clean before he begins his disrupting and enticing work. Quite the opposite. By honestly facing what is happening in our relationships, by admitting deep pain in our souls and the strategies we use to preserve ourselves against it, and by meaningfully confessing our doubts about God's goodness, we are exposed to the ugly

The Fallen Structure	Three Spheres of Experience	The Story of Our Lives	
Fifth Floor Fourth Floor	Here's how! I will survive!	Approach to relationships	Our present story
Third Floor Second Floor First Floor	I hate me I hate you I need you	Antidote against pain	Our inside story
Foundation	I doubt God	Attitude toward God	Our deepest story

passions that rule us and are aroused by the deeper thirst within us that will draw us to Christ.

Our part in the process of being exposed and aroused is to tell the story of our lives to one another in the deliberate consciousness that God is present.

Look at the diagram above and think for a moment about the fallen structure I described in Part II. Notice that the six elements making up that structure naturally divide into three *spheres of experience*, three parts of the story of our lives.

The fourth and fifth floors ("I Will Survive" and "Here's How I Will Survive") combine to describe our *approach to relationships*, our present story.

The first, second, and third floors ("I Need You," "I Hate You," and "I Hate Me") deal with our *antidote for pain*, the inside story of how we defend against the harm others do to us.

And the foundation ("I Doubt God") reveals our *attitude toward God*, the deepest story of our lives.

Moving through our problems toward finding God requires us to tell the story of our lives in a way that disrupts our contentment with each element in the fallen structure and awakens those deep longings in our hearts that make us pant after God.

19
Telling Our Stories

I struggle with a problem I have made known to only one other person. That person's acceptance of me in spite of my problem has created a deep bond. With several others, I have shared a variety of other intensely personal concerns that with all my heart I wish were resolved but aren't.

It seems so terribly obvious that the very best thing someone could do for me would be to help me overcome my problems, especially the one that plagues me most.

Yesterday, Anna wept as she described her marriage. Richard is a cruel, vindictive husband who clothes his destroying power with warm words that cut sharply into Anna's soul. With self-righteous passion, he defends his authoritarian, mean-spirited treatment of her as his expression of biblical headship over a rebellious wife. Anna, of course, is not guiltless, but her heart is open to the Spirit's work. Judging from everything I can see, his is not.

If my daughter were married to this man, I would do whatever I could to improve the situation. It would be difficult to honor any higher value than relief from the daily assaults

Anna endures on her already battered soul. It seems so terribly obvious that the very best thing someone could do for her would be to give her a changed husband or get her away from the one she has.

Marilyn and Roger's twenty-nine years of marriage were troubled: frequent tensions, chronic money problems, struggles with faith, and regular separation required by his work. Then things changed. Everything seemed to come together for them. They fell in love all over again. He accepted a position requiring almost no travel at a higher salary than he had ever made. One night, as he held his wife, he wept with joy and said, "God is so good. I've never felt more in his will than right now." Two hours later, he died from a heart attack.

It seems so terribly obvious that the best thing someone could have done would have been to give this couple more years to enjoy one another.

One Wednesday evening after choir practice, Carol, a middle-aged single woman, walked alone to her car in the church parking lot. A sixteen-year-old boy emerged from the shadows, forced her into her car at gunpoint, made her drive to a deserted spot in the woods, and for the next twenty-four hours coerced her to engage in vile and perverted sexual activity. He then left the car and ran off.

In a professional office two days later, a therapist asked her to relive the horrors of that day by visualizing, with closed eyes, all that happened, but to imagine Jesus there with her. The technique was meant to heal Carol's painful memory. Instead, she immediately lost control and screamed, "That's just the problem. I already believe he was there. Why didn't he do anything?"

It seems so terribly obvious that the very best thing someone could have done would have been to arrange for someone to accompany Carol into that parking lot.

God has the power to halt my struggle, to change Anna's husband, to postpone heart attacks, and to prevent the attacks of deviant young men hiding in the bushes. Does he care? Is he good?

Marilyn is now a widow, living every day with the relentless pain of loneliness and with unanswered questions that tear into her soul. Carol cannot escape haunting memories nor fully recover from unerasable scars. Both women turned to God for . . . what?

WHAT IS GOD DOING?

Sometimes it's hard to know what God is doing. He informs us that he withholds nothing good from his children. I take that to mean that *there is nothing that perfect goodness coupled with absolute power should be doing that isn't being done— right now!*

Yet I still do battle with a problem I hate. Anna's husband continues to chew up her heart. The ache in the widow's heart remains. The abused woman can't sleep. Tomorrow another airplane will crash. A physician will glumly tell someone you love, "There's nothing I can do." A young man, when he learns his fiancée has been sexually abused, will say, "I don't think it's God's will that I marry you." Another Christian leader—this time one you really believed in—will have an affair.

We all rage at God, demanding he do more than he is doing. He remains quietly unthreatened, saddened beyond words that we think him cruel or indifferent, but unswervingly committed to the course he has set. He refuses to redesign the plot of the book, having already written the last chapter and knowing that the ending is very, very good, and that every thread in our story is necessary to that conclusion.

We all rage at God, demanding he do more than he is doing.

As I rage at him in the middle of my pain, he replies with an invitation to live as he lived, to give, to be, and to worship.

And with what appears to be callous insensitivity to all that is happening in my life, he says, "Come, find me. Don't wait for your problems to go away. Get to know me. Let your soul delight in the richest of fare."

"But God," I quickly retort, "getting to know you isn't really what I'm after. Don't you see? I can't endure what's happening in my life. And God, poor Anna! You've got to get her out of that mess. I couldn't endure one hour what she endures every day."

"You could endure it with joy if you knew how good I am," he replies. "You want me to prove my goodness on your terms. But if I yield to your demand, you will not *trust* me; you will rather come to think you *own* me. I will do something more necessary to your eventual happiness than solving your problems. I will let you discover my infinite goodness so that you can rest joyfully in your relationship with me, even though problems will continue until I move you into the better place I'm preparing for you."

An elderly retired pastor approached me after a service where I had preached on unanswered questions in the Christian's life. He was a short, thin man with a clear mind and a passion I could feel as he spoke. He put his hand on my shoulders, looked up at me with an intense, gentle stare, and said: "I am eighty-seven years old. I lost my wife four years ago. I have never known such pain. I have begged God to take it away, to give me a sense of his presence that would ease this terrible loneliness I feel. He has not done so. But he has given me a taste of his goodness. I have a glimpse of what he has in store for me. And I am content till I go home."

I cannot imagine the anguish in that man's soul as he sits alone at the breakfast table. He still hurts, but he is moving through his problems toward finding God. And God has revealed himself to him: he continues to live with meaning and joy in the midst of pain.

IS GOD REALLY GOOD?

Is God really good? That is the question beneath all our other questions about life, a question that must sometimes be screamed. I see pictures of starving children and tortured men in the newspapers—and I want to turn the page. I want to check out the football scores. Read the comics. I don't want to believe that the same God who is doing nothing to improve these people's situation is in charge of my life, the lives of my two sons, and that of my wife and my aging parents.

The words of Christ sometimes feel like sadistic mockery, teasing me with what I long for but can't experience: "Be of good cheer," he says.

"Why, Lord?" I cry.

"Because I have overcome the world."

"But look at China, look at my friends in the Philippines, look at Anna, look at me! What on earth do you mean when you say that you've overcome the world. Things are a mess!"

"If you look for evidence of my goodness in what you see around you and inside you, you will reach a terribly wrong conclusion. You will conclude that sometimes I am good and sometimes I am not. But if you look for evidence of my goodness in the way things will be one day, if you are willing to believe that I am at work now to prepare for that day, and if you ponder the meaning of my death, then you will realize that all the badness in the world—including Anna's husband, your private problem (which I've known about before you confided in your friend), and the starving children in Somalia—can no more conquer my goodness than a child can outwrestle a man.

"To the degree that you develop confidence in my goodness, you will be able to live as I have lived. While I hung on the cross, I was looking out for others, not myself. I defended against nothing; I simply expressed my love for my Father and my commitment to his plan. And I never violated the requirements for worship. You can learn to do it, too, in the middle of your unresolved problems."

BUILDING UP A GODLY STRUCTURE

Sometimes the message breaks through. When it does, nothing matters more than finding Christ and becoming more like him. And as a passion to give suffocates selfishness, I find release from the pressure to be what I am not. As doubt yields to worshipful confidence in God's goodness, that wretched fallen structure weakens and totters and eventually falls. Those problems that draw their energy from my demand that life work as I think it should slowly recede.

A godly structure emerges. We sense the beginnings of an intactness, a solid identity and purpose, that make it less important that people like us. But what can I do to make that happen more often and more deeply? How will it happen in my life, in Anna's life, in your life?

The answer extends beyond the obviously necessary requirements that we spend time in prayer, in the Word, in Christian fellowship, and in service. Those requirements must become opportunities for encountering God, or they are nothing. And the answer lies beyond the catch-all suggestion to "get counseling." It demands supernatural resources that we can never manipulate, only trust.

CONVERSATIONS THAT DISTURB AND ENTICE

Moving through our problems toward finding God requires a fresh understanding of community and a courageous willingness to enter it. We must learn how to talk with one another so that the object of our conversation is to *disturb* each other with how manipulative, defensive, and self-serving we are. Our conversation must also *entice* us to influence others for good, to enjoy our uniqueness, and to rest fully in the goodness of God, no matter what happens.

When community is working, tensions may seem unresolvable and pressures overwhelming, but the opportunity to find God will remain if we stay involved. We must not yield to the urge to retreat into the silence of safe, superficial chatter. We must keep talking. And our words must matter. They must reveal what is most shamefully true about us.

The richest conversations always tell a story. Each of our lives is a dramatic story of how a relational, passionate, thoughtful, purposeful, and depraved person handles the experience of life. Woven into our story will always be the tragedy of our using people, our defending ourselves against them, and our worshiping ourselves. The fallen structure within each of us sees to that.

But the indelible stamp of our Savior insures that the story will also include a tale of noble aspiration, usually in an almost unrecognizable subplot, but still undeniably present. Those good passions, whether smothered beneath bad ones that rule us or released to become a driving force, are neither effective nor commendable until they draw their energy from a confidence in God's goodness.

Both the storyteller and the listener need to hear the doubting soul struggling to find an identity. They need to look eagerly for the movement of God that frees people to give, to be, and to worship. Typically, conversations that lead us toward a deeper awareness of God first disrupt, then entice.

Most interactions should be pleasant ("Hi! How are you?"), functional ("Would you pick me up at the airport?"), or important ("As elders, we need to decide how we're going to deal with this disturbing news.") No one is quite so irritating as the junior counselor who turns normal conversations into therapy sessions. Uninvited probing into motives and weighty expressions of concern spoil pleasant, functional, and important conversations.

But good community does include meaningful moments when the quality of our relationships with God, others, and ourselves is discussed. Each of us has friends who know us well and care about us, friends who live honestly enough to wrestle with unanswered questions. With those friends, we need to risk a level of self-disclosure that makes us uncomfortable.

During lunch with a good friend, you may sense a desire to mention the difficult problems you are facing with your son. Ask your friend if she would be willing to listen to your family concerns. As you tell your story, be sure to focus more on the way you relate to your son than on his problems. Are you critical, overbearing, too easily controlled?

If there aren't times when
the very foundations of our relationships
are torn away and we continue on
only because of Christ, we are not
building strong relationships.

Encourage others to tell their stories to you. Ask questions that require people to think about their experience, to visualize scenes in their lives that provoke deep feelings. "What was it like for you to walk into that hospital room?" "What did you say to yourself when your father told you he was divorcing your mother?" "Who did you most enjoy telling the good news about your new job?"

Good conversations are often disturbing. They deal with the edge in someone's voice that puts others on guard. They face up to the pain that a friend's snub or a parent's neglect has provoked. Good conversations uncover the terror and rage that often lie hidden beneath a veneer of comfortable relationship. If there aren't times when the very foundations of our relationships are torn away and we continue on only because of Christ, we are not building strong relationships.

HONEST STORYTELLERS

Let me illustrate the process I want to describe in these last chapters, the process of finding God in a community of honest storytellers.

I work with six colleagues. We all like and respect each

other; but we are seven imperfect, sometimes petty, occasionally bizarre men whose love for God is not yet strong enough to keep our depraved urges completely controlled.

We meet weekly for two hours. Recently, I came to a meeting with heavy burdens that I wasn't handling well. My mood was angry and despairing. I chose not to make known my troubles, but the other men quickly sensed my dark mood.

And yet it was never discussed. No one aggressively questioned me or consoled me or confronted me. And I never openly admitted the obvious fact that I was carrying a heavy weight. I never invited them to discuss my concerns.

We struggled to fill the time: business was handled, opinions were voiced, humor was offered, but none of us addressed the irritating and stifling effect of my mood on the group. I ended the meeting by announcing that I was no longer willing to attend pointless meetings where nothing of substance was discussed. I instructed anyone who had a definite agenda for next week's meeting to distribute a memo stating his agenda and to come prepared to direct the time. Otherwise there would be no meeting. My last words were, "I'd rather stay in bed than get up for no purpose."

The tension was thick as we filed out of the room. Everyone was mad. I felt both offended (not one person directly probed to see what was going on inside me) and self-righteous (meetings should have a clear time-redeeming purpose). For a time, I was buoyed by indignation.

That night I wanted to quit. The earlier angry despair sank into nihilism. I could see no point in working with these men, or with anybody. They were good men—I knew I could find none better—but we had no community. I knew it was partly my fault, partly theirs. But I could not exactly identify either the problem or the solution. I could talk about my anger, but I had done that before. Like so many others in similar seasons of relational tension, I saw no profit in airing the problems. Things seemed hopeless. I wanted out.

With these thoughts swirling through my mind, I went to

bed. I couldn't sleep. I tossed and turned. I prayed. I begged God to give me a taste of himself, to make me aware of his presence, to restore a sense of mission and strength to my life.

But nothing came. The heavens were silent. The Spirit, I now believe, was grieved by my cowardly pride. God would not let me find him if I continued in justifying my isolation from my brothers. Finding God and living in community are tied together. You cannot pursue one without pursuing the other. Desperate prayer, disciplined fasting, and hours in the Word will not persuade God to reveal himself when we ignore relational tensions. "Whoever loves his brother lives in the light . . . but whoever hates his brother . . . walks around in the darkness; . . . the darkness has blinded him" (1 John 2:10–11).

Within a few days, one of the men told us that he had an agenda for the next meeting. I didn't want to attend, but the condition I imposed for regathering was met. I showed up. All of us did. Except one—he was sick. I envied him.

After the agenda was presented, I turned to the one presenting it and pointedly said that I felt he was pulling away from me, and that the plans outlined in his agenda reflected that movement. I told two others that I sensed a spirit of competition developing between us regarding a ministry they were pursuing that paralleled one that I was doing.

I knew I was dropping bombs. As soon as I dropped them, however, an emergency phone call pulled me away and ended the meeting.

We met again five days later. We agreed to explore openly the impact we were having on one another. I call that *telling our present story*. We moved from the immediate issues of conflict into a discussion of how our styles of relating were provoking strong feelings.

One of the men with whom I felt a spirit of competition stated that I had badly used him. I never knew he felt that way and was unaware of what I had done to contribute to those feelings. We went back and forth discussing the matter for some time. Eventually, I became aware of something stirring in me, something beneath my defensive explanations for what I had done. I loved this man. And I had hurt him. When I admitted that to myself, I felt deeply grieved. Something changed inside me. Nothing seemed more important than my desire to treat him well. I put into words the energy stirring within me. It was a good moment, but not complete.

The desire to love him better, once expressed, opened a door to deeper parts within me. I hadn't intended to use my friend and I felt hurt by his lack of trust. I felt alone and hopeless. As I verbalized those concerns, I was beginning to *tell my inside story*, the tale of a man who longs for what he has never received. I put it this way: "I feel important to many, but liked by few."

Another colleague prompted more of my inside story by saying that of the ten most important sentences ever said to him, I had spoken five. As he spoke, I trembled with pain. "That's just the problem," I said. "I'm valued for my ability to help, but no one thinks of me when it's time to have fun."

With that sentence, my mind was flooded with hard memories: the party to which I was not invited, thrown by a couple who told me I had saved their marriage. Everyone in our social circle was invited but my wife and me. Why? Another memory came: the time after an unusually dramatic counseling session held in front of my counseling students when dozens of people flocked about the counselee while I walked slowly out of the room, drained, unnoticed, alone.

But even as I felt the crushing weight of aloneness, a strange exhilaration rushed through me. I can only describe it as a sense of being, a thrill of living. I exist. I live in a fallen world where, like every other honest person, I feel alone, but I am alive with something to offer. No pain or damage can rob me of that. By the miracle of grace, I can go on as a person committed to a far higher purpose than relieving loneliness. And I can face my weaknesses and hurts, and be moved by the affection that sometimes comes my way.

But it isn't enough. It never will be. My colleagues felt my pain. The compassion in their hearts was visible in their eyes. I felt for them. They felt for me. But in the middle of rich unity, we began to realize, perhaps with new force, the insufficiency of our love for one another.

And that awareness led to *telling our deepest story.* We were silenced by our need for a purpose larger than ourselves. All our burdens and jealousies seemed petty in comparison to a big picture that was emerging with clarity. We needed to relate with someone who is telling a larger story than any of us could see, and who could help us to move through still unresolved tensions toward a goal that by its sheer vastness dwarfed all other objectives.

We began talking about our commitment to God. No other topic seemed to matter. We felt small, but hopeful. Worship seemed to spread through the room. We were impressed with God. After a time of savoring the sweet fragrance of worship, we ended the meeting. A few decisions had been made. We had faced significant tensions but did not resolve them. But we left with a renewed desire to give to one another, to offer our unique contributions to the body of Christ, and to live for the glory of Someone beyond ourselves.

We had told our *present story* of mutual failure and hurt until conviction broke open our hearts and released our *passion to give.* We told our *inside story* of disappointment and loneliness until pain gave way to a *passion to be.* And we told our *deepest story* of a longing to rest in another's strength until we fell into worship.

DEVELOPING GODLY PASSION

God reveals himself to people whose passion to know him makes them supremely uncomfortable with whatever grieves or offends him, not only because they fear reprisal but far more because they long for intimacy. Godly passion develops when we face what is true about the way we relate to others, including God, and yearn to relate differently. The exposure of bad ruling passions and the surfacing of good dormant passions most powerfully occurs as we tell our stories to one another in the presence of God, deliberately choosing to be open to his work of shattering and rebuilding.

When we tell our *present story*, the story that shows our determination to survive in a world without a good God and our strategy for relating to a world full of disappointing people, we recognize and disrupt the tough shell we have formed around ourselves, and we become enticed by the possibility of meaningful connection with others for their sake.

When we tell our *inside story*, the story that shows our demand that people come through for us because God doesn't and our hatred toward others when they don't, we recognize and disrupt our stubbornness in trying to protect ourselves against what we so deeply fear, and we become enticed by our longing to live without pretense or defensiveness in community.

When we tell our *deepest story*, the story that shows our doubt of God's goodness and our terror and rage when he doesn't come through for us, we get in touch with and disrupt the terror that corrupts our joy and the clench-fisted rage toward a God whose goodness does not guarantee our immediate comfort. And when we enter the reality of our doubt, rage, and terror, we realize with healthy shame how profoundly unbecoming it is to question his love, how desperately we long to trust him, and how difficult—and wicked—it is to call him bad. When we recognize that the core issue is whether we believe he is good, we uncover the foundation of belief that has already been laid in our hearts.

As a friend recently said to me, "When things are tough, I angrily assume that God is bad. But when I admit that that's what I'm saying about him, then I know I don't really believe that. For some reason, it feels powerful to rage against God. But it feels peaceful to acknowledge that he really is good."

At the risk of reducing something as wondrously mysterious and unpredictably fluid as good conversation to a mechani-

	DISRUPT	**ENTICE**
Present Story (Approach to People)	**Self-Centeredness** Hardness, insensitivity; lack of compassion; manipulative agendas; self-centeredness.	**Giving** Impact, blessings; using our resources to impact others for good; longing to see others do well.
Inside Story (Antidote against Pain)	**Self-Protection** Determination to survive; defensive dependency; using internal resources to protect self against pain.	**Being and Growing** Courage to be; to explore self to find uniqueness that can serve a good purpose.
Deepest Story (Attitude toward God)	**Self-Service** Terror of what is true and what may happen; rage at God for not providing better guarantees; doubts of his goodness.	**Worship** Courage to live based on confidence in God's goodness; intimate enjoyment of a God we can trust and to whom we belong.

cal, step-by-step process, let me express these thoughts in the diagram shown above.

Telling our stories takes courage. Exposing the sinful passions that so often rule us requires humility. And letting ourselves feel how bad we want to be an instrument of good in others' lives and to know a source of guidance that will free us to rest will create an intense longing to know him better. We need to risk that he is good by telling our stories. We need to depend on his grace as we face our ugly passions. We need to trust that he will let us find him by entrusting to him the most profound, disappointed passion in our hearts.

20
Stories That Disrupt and Entice

O ur lives consist of routines and responsibilities: coffee brewed automatically at 6:30 every morning; paying bills once a month; lunch every Tuesday with the same friend. We chat, read newspapers, quarrel, shop, eat, watch TV, work, and play. We go to church, attend a weeknight Bible study, pray, listen to gospel music, and buy books from a Christian bookstore. Some of us spend regular time in personal study of the Scripture; we teach Sunday school; we share Christ with unbelieving friends; we sacrifice time and money to serve the Lord.

But very few of us talk to one another. We pour words back and forth, of course—some heated, some gossipy, some endearing, some religious. But we rarely sit and listen to anyone tell their story. At least not for a long time, say for ten or twelve hours over a period of months. If we do tell our stories, we do so to become better acquainted with each other, not to discover God. We tell what we think our listener wants to hear. We reveal what we think will reflect kindly on ourselves. If, however, we told our stories to each other to know Christ more deeply, our stories would be different. Likely they would be far more embarrassing, far more humbling, and far more terrifying.

Therapy groups and self-help meetings encourage an honest, and sometimes lengthy, telling of our stories, with the intent of straightening out twisted lives and encouraging more effective listening habits. But they too easily become narcissism factories, manufacturing bloated egos more concerned with having a satisfying life than with fitting in with God's design.

We in the Christian community need to tell our stories, risking shame and rebuke, because we want to find God. We must keep reading our Bibles and listening to good Bible teachers; we must worship and serve together; we must discipline ourselves to give generously to the Lord's work; we must make Christ known to an unbelieving world. But we must also learn to tell our stories to one another.

TELLING YOUR PRESENT STORY

You must tell your *present story*, the tale of your current relationships, partly to uncover the subtlety and extent of your self-centeredness. Look for self-centeredness in the motives behind your jokes, criticisms, opinions, and silences. Ask others what your impact is on them as you relate together. Be open to admitting self-serving themes in your patterns of relating.

A good friend once told me that he paid a price for my humor. My "friendly" gibe in front of his fiancée embarrassed him. I was forced to admit that I sometimes use humor to cover my insecurity and that such attention-getting maneuvers hurt others.

Maybe you freely compliment others to appear kind and generous, to convince yourself that you're not the selfish person people say you are. Perhaps you rarely express warmth because you're afraid it will not be returned.

As you face these self-focused elements in your style of relating and measure them by God's impossible standard of love, you will notice a queasy feeling arising within you. You can easily ignore or dismiss this feeling with the attitude: "I'm being too hard on myself. I need to like myself better, and this surely isn't helping." Instead, identify that queasy feeling as something good, perhaps corrupted with lots of false guilt and shame, but still good. Something moral within you that calls you to a higher plane of living is being jarred by what you are facing in yourself. Whatever else may be true about you, whatever abuse or tragedy you may have endured, you were called to an other-centered style of relating that you regularly violate.

Let the uneasiness of guilt be the doorway through which your noble passion escapes into awareness. You were built to connect in love just as you were built to breathe. And even though that design has been corrupted, distorted, and smothered under the weight of self-centeredness, the impulse to connect remains within you. If it doesn't, you are beyond the reach of grace.

You long to connect with each of your children, even the one who so badly broke your heart. And beneath the thick mound of rage and hurt, you can detect a tiny spark of desire to see the one who so badly abused you restored to godly living and joy. (You will *not* be disappointed to see that person in heaven. Recovery from terrible mistreatment is never meaningful until the victim hungers for the restoration of the abuser and is even willing to be an instrument of that restoration.)

When a song, a sermon, or a movie penetrates the crust of your soul and releases your passion to bless, connect, and love, you will be immediately overwhelmed with the sheer impossibility of acting on that passion without help. Let that profound realization drive you to Christ, who wants you to love as he loves. Feel the urgency within you to know Christ better.

Now, when you are aware of your self-centeredness and your longing to connect by loving others (including those who have hurt you), you will seek God with more of your heart. And your desire to know God as *forgiver* and *enabler* will help you resist temptation, spend more time in Scripture, discipline yourself to pray, and worship regularly.

TELLING YOUR INSIDE STORY

Then continue your pursuit of God by telling your *inside story*. Explore your history and your heart with a commitment to pretend about nothing. Tell the story of your childhood, not to shift blame or to find yourself, but rather to admit the turmoil and rage and fear that grew in you over a long series of disappointments. You may have wonderful parents, but even the best have let you down. Chances are high that your parents are the source of your deepest, most shattering pain.

Perhaps if you learn to honor your parents, you will find yourselves equipped to handle all other relationships.

It is no accident that the fifth commandment to honor your parents stands at the beginning of the six commandments that have to do with human relationships. It stands before the commandments that address your relationship with your spouse, children, and friends. Why? Perhaps if you learn what it means to honor your parents, you will find yourselves equipped to handle all other relationships.* Perhaps the greatest challenge to belief in God's goodness (a belief necessary for loving others well) is the universal and often severe failure of parents to provide well for a vulnerable, easily damaged child.

Admit the hurt, anger, and fear in your soul that began years ago and continues today. Embrace them as enemies that can be used for a good purpose. Replay the events in your history that stand out as especially difficult or joyful, or perhaps

---

*I am indebted to my friend Bill Odoumolon, pastor of Foothills Bible Church in Denver, Colorado, for this insight.

simply intense and hard to forget. Spend time reflecting on those memories with a few good friends.

You may find yourself engulfed by strong emotions that you have never felt so deeply before. Some of those emotions will be ugly. Keep in mind that the root of ugly emotion does not lie in how others have treated you, but rather in your demand that they treat you well. Admit that demand—then face how that demand has fed a hatred for all those who have let you down. Explore whether you have handled disappointment by taking a strong kick at yourself for not being worthy of better treatment. If so, you are now filled with self-contempt.

Notice how hard you work to protect yourself from more pain and to preserve whatever self-esteem still remains. As you enter your inside world and find it filled with an angry passion to survive, you may think nothing else is there. But there is. Look for a quiet urge within you simply to live, to rest, to go about your business without having to prove or protect yourself against anything, to enjoy existence, your existence, at its deepest level. You want to live honestly, peacefully, happily.

But you can't. There's too much danger of failure and rejection to stop scrambling, to relax, to live. No one in their right mind would expect to enjoy a casual stroll through a city at war. You are determined to survive a world filled with snipers who fire insults, assassins who abuse, and undercover agents who win your confidence then stab you in the back. And you may be surviving well. You may have become so skilled at survival that you really are enjoying the power of your success.

The real enemy—doubt of God—remains hidden. Secretly, it establishes a beachhead in your demanding determination that others come through for you. Doubting God is a far more serious problem than whatever mistreatment you have endured: it is the root of all sin.

As you expose your demanding spirit, you will soon experience a passion to rest, to make no demands because you trust the one in charge, to live in an environment where you feel safe to develop your potential rather than always to stay on guard against danger. You will more clearly see that you must live consciously in the presence of a reliable refuge in whose strength you are free to live your life rather than attempt to hang onto it. The desire to know God as *protector* and *liberator* will grow within you. And you will seek him with more of your heart.

TELLING YOUR DEEPEST STORY

Too often, people stop there, if in fact they get this far. They tend to look no further than at their *present story* of self-centeredness and a longing to connect, and at their *inside story* that reveals both their defensiveness and their passion to live. They assume that learning more responsible patterns of relating and gaining clearer insights into their emotional makeup will move them along toward maturity.

But it won't. Neither your present story nor your inside story exposes the core problem. You must tell the *deepest story* of your life, the tale of suspicion, terror, and rage that emerges from your attitude toward God.

Four key questions can guide your telling of this story:

1. *What difference does God's love make in your life?*

Are you resting confidently in the care of a God who has given you no guarantees of good health, a faithful spouse, obedient children, or an adequate income? Do you live with the nagging fear that something terrible might happen tomorrow, something you won't be able to handle? Is God a source of deep comfort although he sovereignly arranged for you to be born to an alcoholic mother and allowed you to be molested by her third husband? When you are in the middle of intolerable pain, is there a joy beneath the suffering because you know that God's goodness will one day swallow up all the badness in life?

2. Are you grateful for God's help as you face the difficult decisions of life?

Have you learned that God's style of leadership does not relieve you of the responsibility to make courageous decisions in the middle of confusion? Have you found out that God does not always make clear the particulars of what he wants you to do? Is that okay with you? Or does that frustrate you?

When you have no idea how to repair a fractured relationship or what job you should take, does the Bible come alive as a treasured source of God's wisdom, or do you lay it aside in disgust because you can find no verse that tells you exactly what to do? Are you resting in the confidence that somehow God is always at work in your life? Or does the story of a friend of yours, who prayed for wisdom then made a decision that led to great suffering, unnerve you a bit?

3. Are you trusting in God's power to heal in spite of deep wounds that still remain in your soul?

Are you demanding that God heal your wounds before you will rest in his power to heal? Have you found a healing that releases you to love others better, or do you find superficial healing through self-affirmation and boundary setting? Which offends you more—your ongoing pain, or your ongoing sin? Which do you value more—healing or forgiveness?

Which offends you more—your ongoing pain, or your ongoing sin?

Has your search for healing made the cross into an affirmation of your value more than an atonement for your sins? And has this same search brought you into contact, not with the God who frees you to love in the middle of continued suffering, but rather with a fake god, a narcotic that dulls your pain but never builds your character?

4. Have you had a taste of God that stirs passion within you deeper than all others, including the passions for sexual pleasure, personal fulfillment, and relief from pain?

Has God revealed himself to you in a way that, at least for a moment, made sin unthinkable and utterly unattractive? Has your experience of God created a compassion for your bitterest enemies? Has your realization that God is the point, and not you, freed you to keep caring about others when you are badly hurting?

GLIMPSES OF GLORY

These questions may help you to tell your *deepest story* in a way that uncovers the rage, terror, and doubts of God's goodness that may still linger in your soul. When you admit how terrified you are of life, how angry you sometimes feel toward God when he fails to protect you from pain, and how often you question his goodness, you are again disrupted, this time more than ever.

The square pegs of rage, terror, and doubt do not fit the round shape of your soul. You were built to enjoy love, rest, and trust. And as you admit your rage, terror, and doubt, a passion begins to emerge, a passion to make it on your own no longer, a passion to be consumed with the wonder of Christ, a passion to know him as Lord. It is then that you learn what it means to seek God with all your heart, to come to him believing that he is all that Christ revealed him to be and that he is the rewarder of all those who earnestly seek him. And it is then that the glimpses come, at unpredictable times and in unexpected forms, but they come.

And when they come, the mystery deepens. You are less tempted to retreat to formulas that are supposed to persuade God to transfigure himself before you. God remains absolutely independent, disclosing himself when he chooses. But now his unpredictability becomes delightful, simply because you have seen him. You know what he is like. You trust him to do whatever is good because you know he is good. As long as this confidence remains, you experience a peace beneath your worst trial, an eagerness to love in spite of mistreatment, and a joy deeper than your deepest sorrow.

You still struggle, sometimes severely, with fear, anger, and discouragement. But now a quiet awareness will not fully go away, an awareness that God is good, that sin is bad, and that the relief it brings is temporary and, in the long run, futile. You find yourself a little more patient. You check irritability when it rises. You are confident, even in the middle of panic, that things will be all right. You actually begin to believe the Lord when he says, "But take heart! I have overcome the world" (John 16:33). You rest in the guarantee that all the badness in the world will never overcome God's goodness. The last chapter, the one that never ends, will be the story of goodness reaching into every part of life: reunions of unparalleled joy, relationships without selfishness, work without pressure, travel without accidents, and the pure laughter of people having a really *good* time.

Can you imagine what it will be like to enjoy perfect confidence in God in a world with absolutely no trials, no mistreatment, and no sorrow? "Everyone who has this hope in him purifies himself" (1 John 3:3) by obeying the commands of Christ. And he who obeys them, "he is the one who loves me . . . and I too will love him and *show myself to him*"(John 14:21, italics mine). We are called to move through our problems toward *finding God*. "'You will seek me and find me when you seek me with all your heart. I will be found by you,' declares the LORD" (Jer. 29:13).

21
Coming Home Again

I t is right to think hard about life, to probe into the complexities of your relationship with yourself and others. But you must conduct these adventures of thought in the same spirit as children explore their grandfather's old, rambling house. Seemingly endless closets and crevices and corners in the attic dare children to leave the well-lit living room where grandfather always sits; but that living room is headquarters, and the children are careful to keep the way back clearly in mind.

Many Christians today have courageously ventured into the dark regions of the soul but have forgotten the way back to the room where the eternal Father gathers his children onto his lap and reads stories to them by the fireplace. They feel very grown-up when they talk about sexual abuse and multiple personality disorders. The almost rebellious excitement that comes from moving farther away from the living room makes them feel quite superior to those who are still relaxing by the cozy fire, listening to childish tales about walls falling down and stones from a slingshot killing a giant.

The danger in thinking hard about the problems of life is not that you will discover elements that your faith cannot handle; it is rather that you may think you have entered uncharted territory where the simplicity of Christ cannot provide adequate light. You assume that you need special knowledge to help the woman with a history of satanic ritual abuse and the Christian teacher who for years has fondled little girls.

Is it possible that your great need is not for more understanding of ritual abuse or sexual addiction but rather for richer and more powerful wisdom about what it means to know God? Could there be a dimension to knowing Christ that effectively addresses all the root causes beneath the problems with which you struggle?

THE LAST WORD

God knows everything about you. He is thoroughly aware of all the personal struggles that threaten to undo you. He knows your history and your present life, all of it. And all he says to you is, "Christ." In previous days, God distributed bits and pieces of information, and he gave it to us in a variety of ways. But now he tells us that everything he made known earlier is more fully revealed in Christ. That is his final speech: "Christ!" There is no more to say.

"In the past God spoke to our forefathers through the prophets at many times and in various ways, but in these last days he has spoken to us by his Son, whom he appointed heir of all things, and through whom he made the universe" (Heb. 1:1–2).

God wants you to sit by the fire and listen to the Spirit read sixty-six books that tell all about him. And when you think about a friend struggling with homosexual desires, he wants you to leave the living room and go to the attic where that person is telling his story, but to return quickly with your friend so both of you can listen to a far better story.

The deepest, most profoundly relevant truths are always the simple ones. Paul was grateful for the Thessalonian's *work of faith*, *labor of love*, and *patience of hope*. Jesus told us that the work of God was to believe in the One whom God sent. And that means to develop confidence in his character. God really is good. Look at Christ. Christ makes that clear. He gives us faith.

The labor of love is to serve Christ, to make him known by treating others the way he treats them, by living life as he has lived it. And the patience of hope keeps our attention fixed on the city yet to come. Instead of trying to build a city here, we look forward to the one that he is constructing in a better place.

To believe Christ (faith), to serve Christ (love), and to wait for Christ (hope): that is what it means to find God.

But to the degree that you haven't found him, your passions are out of control. Trust is out. You want to *explain* and *control*; therefore, you reduce mystery to manageable categories and attempt to run your own life without depending on Christ.

You like to *be right*. You call it earnestly contending for the faith, and you persuade yourself that you are God's ally in defending truth. But your angry spirit of smugness and condescension gives you away. Compassion and humility yield to arrogance.

You long to *heal*, to relieve pain. But when that becomes a higher priority than worship, you create a god who suits your humane purpose, and you devote your life to helping people feel better about themselves. You end up using a false god rather than worshiping the true One.

You long to *connect* with the supernatural. You embrace mystery, fall prostrate before God in humility, and yield yourself to no higher purpose than experiencing him. But your focus is on *experience*. You demand it. So you come up with methods to get it. Eventually, you become more caught up with your theology of finding God and the evidence that you have done so than with God himself.

To every cry from your passion-filled hearts, God replies, "Christ."

Let your *passion to explain* become a *passion to know Christ* and all that he reveals through the book that God wrote about him. Think hard, explore, take risks in your ideas, talk to people about their lives, but never leave the chair by the fire for very long. Let your work of faith be always to believe he is good.

Let your *passion to be right* become a *passion to honor Christ* in all that you do. Study hard, dialogue, debate, but always do it in a way that helps others to see how kind and good God really is. Let warm conviction replace cold dogmatism. Let your labor of love be to reflect God's character always.

Let your *passion to heal* become a *passion to give hope.* The wounds won't all go away now. No method or group or counselor can completely heal them. But you can continue on, doing the work of faith and carrying out the labor of love, even though you are still wounded. A better city awaits you. With the patience of hope, serve faithfully now because you know what lies ahead. Don't wait for your wounds to be healed before you serve.

Dialogue and debate, but always do it in a way that helps others to see how kind and good God really is. Let warm conviction replace cold dogmatism.

Let your *passion to connect* become a *passion to trust* a sovereign Christ who will do for you exactly what needs to be done. He will reveal the Father in his time and in his way in response to your work of faith, labor of love, and patience of hope.

Most of us are crawling about in a stuffy attic, trying to explain life, demanding to be right, doing our best to relieve pain, and wondering where God is. It is time to find our way back to the living room and into the Father's arms, where we can listen to his Spirit tell the story of Christ.

Epilogue

My journey is only beginning. More than ever, I believe I'm on the path to finding God. It is a path of jarring surprises and unsolvable difficulties that requires more faith than I ever thought necessary.

It has been more than two years since I cried out to God for a clearer glimpse of Christ. That prayer has been answered. But not without cost.

I have not experienced a more difficult period in my life than these last two years. At times I have felt inwardly tortured, once to the point where I believe I caught a glimpse of hell.

On the day I completed this book, I did something I've never done before. I got in my car and drove off, having no idea where I was going. If I had confidence in Lourdes, I would have gone there. I think I understand a little of the desperation of pilgrims who cross seas and climb mountains in search of peace.

I found myself on a mountain pass. I parked overlooking some of the richest beauty of God's creation. The beauty both mocked me and enticed me. I felt lost and undone but also beckoned.

As I had done two years earlier, I again cried out to God, but this time with different words: "Lord, unless you reveal yourself to me in a way that draws me to you more than to anyone or anything else, I'd rather die."

The next day, the phone rang. A friend gave me totally unexpected and thoroughly unwelcome news that severely affected my financial situation. Through a series of miscalculations, I owed a great deal of money when I thought some was coming in. I've received far worse news before, but this became an instant symbol for all that I was clinging to in life and for my determined efforts to keep my life in order. After five minutes of controlled panic, I knew that God was holding out to me the opportunity to take the next step—a big one—in my spiritual journey. The message from God seemed clear. "You cannot control your life. You are therefore free. You are not trapped by the need to arrange things as you want. Trust me more fully than you ever have before. Do what I am leading you to do, even though the risks from your perspective are enormous. I am thoroughly good, and I am good enough to trust thoroughly."

I am making plans right now to take the step that God has placed before me. I've already taken it in my heart. Panic is giving way to the terror of trust. A quiet sense of adventure—almost a thrill—is replacing the despairing boredom.

The world is too bad a place—and far too uncertain—to build a home and to count on enjoying it. But it's a perfect place to find God.

About the Author

D r. Larry Crabb is the founder and director of the Institute of Biblical Counseling, a ministry committed to training Christians to resolve life's problems biblically and to help others in the context of Christian community.

In addition to conducting IBC seminars across the country, Dr. Crabb is professor in the Department of Biblical Counseling at Colorado Christian University in Morrison, Colorado.

Dr. Crabb earned his Ph.D. in clinical psychology from the University of Illinois in 1970. He practiced psychology for ten years, and for seven years directed the master's program in biblical counseling at Grace Theological Seminary in Winona Lake, Indiana.

Finding God is Dr. Crabb's eighth book. *Basic Principles of Biblical Counseling* was published in 1975, followed by *Effective Biblical Counseling, The Marriage Builder, Encouragement: The Key to Caring* (with Dan Allender), *Understanding People, Inside Out,* and *Men & Women.*

Dr Crabb and his wife, Rachael, live in Morrison, Colorado. They have two sons, Keplen and Kenton.